A Forty-niner from Tennessee

. . . . .

A Forty-niner

Edited by

· · · · ·

EDWARD M. STEEL

from Tennessee

The Diary of

· · · · ·

Hugh Brown

· · · · ·

Heiskell

· · · · ·

The University of Tennessee Press / Knoxville

LIBRARY OF CONGRESS CATALOGING-IN-PUBLICATION DATA

Heiskell, Hugh Brown, 1826–1849.
A forty-niner from Tennessee : the diary of Hugh Brown
Heiskell / edited by Edward M. Steel. — 1st ed.
p. cm.
Includes bibliographical references and index.
ISBN 1-57233-011-2 (cl.: alk. paper)
1. Heiskell, Hugh Brown, 1826–1849—Diaries.
2. Pioneer—West (U.S.)—Diaries. 3. West (U.S.)—
Description and travel. 4. Overland journeys to the Pacific.
5. California—Gold discoveries. 6. West (U.S.)—
Biography. 7. Knoxville Region (Tenn.)—Biography.
I. Steel, Edward M. II. Title.
F593.H45 1998
979.4'03'092—dc21
[B] 97-45370

• • • • •

To Barbara

Contents

. . . . .

Illustrations
. . . . .
Figures

· · · · ·
Maps

Acknowledgments

· · · · ·

I am grateful to the rangers of the National Park Service and the U. S. Forest Service for maps and directions that enabled me to locate many of the camping places of Hugh Heiskell and his companions. My thanks are also due to the staffs of the Nevada State Museum, Carson City; the Nevada Historical Society, Reno; the Mormon Station State Historic Park, Genoa, Nevada; the Churchill County Museum and Archives, Fallon, Nevada; and interested people along the way from Green River, Wyoming, to Placerville, California, who filled in my knowledge of local areas, especially the El Dorado County Historical Museum and the El Dorado County Public Library, Placerville, California.

My greatest debt is to my wife, Barbara Manley Steel, who shared equally in much of the editorial work and without whose assistance and support the book would not have been completed.

Prologue
. . . . .

HUGH BROWN HEISKELL AND THE
FORTY-NINER ADVENTURE

During a trip overland from Tennessee to the California gold fields in 1849, Hugh Brown Heiskell of Knoxville kept a diary. This edited version comes from his original journal, which he wrote in a leather-bound ledger, and begins with the entry for 13 August at a camp on Green River in present-day Wyoming. The last entry is for 21 October, when he was making his way down to the gold fields from the crest of the Sierra Nevada, among the last travelers to cross the Sierra in 1849. It is one of more than 130 known journals kept by travelers to California in the first year of the gold rush. These journals, many of which have been printed, have supplied basic source material for writers who have explored various aspects of the remarkable forty-niner migration. Each contributes its part to the story so often retold for the past century and a half, but Hugh Heiskell's page-long entries for each day are far more detailed than the majority of his fellow diarists. Like them, he was aware of participating in a historic movement, but he was concerned about keeping a personal record of events for himself, family, and friends.[1]

Hugh Brown Heiskell left few papers that have been preserved, but a family history written by his niece, Eliza Wallace, and letters in various manuscript collections supply some background. He was born in Knoxville, Tennessee, 13 February 1826, the fifth of the ten children of Frederick S. and Eliza Brown Heiskell. Almost nothing is known of his early years, which he spent in Knoxville, except that he was part of not only a large nuclear family but also an even larger extended family. He had no less than thirty-four first cousins living within thirty miles, and he is known to have visited some of them for weeks or even months at a time. The availability of a local school in those days before a public system existed appears to have been a major factor in these long visits by the children. Hugh Heiskell's mother referred to him briefly in family letters, and in an undated letter, written perhaps in 1839, she informed her sister Nancy Lincoln that Hugh was attending a school in Knoxville. "Of my generation," wrote his cousin Tyler Heiskell, reminiscing in his old age, "there were a large number born and reared close together, jolly and considered clannish."[2]

When Hugh Heiskell was about ten years old, his father, the owner and editor of the *Knoxville Register,* sold his printing business and bought States View, a twelve-hundred-acre farm about ten miles southwest of Knoxville. He planted extensive orchards and renamed the estate Fruit Hill. There he engaged in general farming but devoted his attention principally to raising blooded horses, cattle, and swine. A flock of sheep supplied wool that was spun and woven into cloth on the farm. A sawmill and a gristmill on the property served the local community.

On this almost self-sufficient estate, Hugh Heiskell grew up along with one elder and two younger brothers and four younger sisters. In a family history, Eliza Wallace, who as a child during the Civil War lived at Fruit Hill, painted an idyllic picture of the home where her uncle Hugh had passed his youth some twenty years earlier. The orchards provided plentiful fruit of many kinds: apples, peaches, pears, cherries, plums, and quinces. The cellar contained not only bins of fruits but also barrels of sauerkraut and sorghum, jars of apple butter and marmalade, and kegs of vinegar and cider. In addition to the usual barns, sheds, cribs, and springhouse, the farm also had a workshop for repairing farm equipment, a saddle house, a kiln for making molasses, an apple-drying establishment, and a carriage house. "There were candle-dippings, carding and spinning, hog-killing and apple-gathering, soap-making and corn shuckings," Eliza Wallace wrote. "As a great treat mother would take us to the flouring mill, a water mill, and the miller, Hy Hackney, was deaf so the going around of the wheels in their noisy career did not bother him. Miss Adaline, his sister, had a loom and wove cloth, with which the numerous slaves on the Heiskell place were clothed."[3]

Hugh Heiskell's boyhood home, Fruit Hill, 1952. Courtesy of McClung Historical Collection, McClung Museum, Knoxville, Tennessee.

A Forty-niner from Tennessee

On his trip to California, Hugh Heiskell profited from the practical lessons of growing up at Fruit Hill, where he could hardly have failed to learn how to take care of farm animals, including a pair of working oxen. In fact, his knowledge of farm affairs was such that when he was twenty-one his father entrusted him with the management of Fruit Hill, jointly with his mother, for six months. In 1847 the voters of Knox County elected Frederick S. Heiskell to the Tennessee legislature as their senator, and the session began during the harvest season. Shortly after the senator departed for Nashville near the end of September, the mill dam at Fruit Hill broke, and Hugh Heiskell was faced with repairing it and building a new millrace while he finished planting the winter wheat and harvested the last of the corn, the two principal crops at Fruit Hill. Two weeks of hard labor saw the mill restored to operation, not only for their use but also the benefit of the neighbors, who also depended on it. In a letter to her husband a month later, Eliza Heiskell summed up the farm operations: "I have postponed writing until I could tell you that our wheat was finished putting in and that I might give a good account of the farming concerns. Hu is making a perfect slave of himself. The race does finely, no leaks and no trouble with it. We expect to finish gathering our corn today—and will have a 'shucking' tonight—and will put it in the crib as fast as possible. Our hogs are fattening."[4]

Although he proved his competence as a manager, Hugh Heiskell had little taste for agricultural pursuits. "Farmers don't often dream," he wrote his sister Margaret, "their sleep is too sound for them," and to be "following a plough, staggering and stumbling over clods all day, is anything but poetry."[5]

Hugh Heiskell studied to become a lawyer, but exactly when or with whom the family letters do not reveal. In fact, the precise extent of his formal education is uncertain. He is listed as a sophomore at East Tennessee University in 1843, but there is no record of his having graduated. By 1849 he had completed his preparation for practicing law.[6] Perhaps he had some intention of combining law and politics, for he shared F. S. Heiskell's interest in the Whig party and ran political errands for his father in Knox County while the latter was absent in Nashville in 1847–48.[7]

It is not clear why Hugh Heiskell became a part of the overland migration that the discovery of gold in California set off. Most of the seventy to a hundred thousand people who went to California in 1849 made their decisions privately, and the relative importance of the hunt for gold, or desire for land, or thirst for adventure were mixed with other ingredients in many different combinations. Hugh Heiskell's

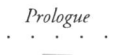

diary makes hardly any reference to his intentions, though a letter to his sister Sue indicates that he expected to return home in a year or two. Many forty-niners, in a contemporary phrase, "went to see the elephant"; that is, they embarked on an adventure to experience life, to gain knowledge even if it meant enduring hard knocks. If they picked up a fortune along the way, so much the better.

If the first part of Hugh Heiskell's journal had been preserved, it might have resolved the question of what drew him to California. At some time someone cut out the twelve pages preceding the first entry in the journal as it now exists. When he began keeping his diary, Hugh may have made some reference to his hopes and intentions. It may also be speculated that these missing pages contained an account of his movements between Tennessee and Green River. A reference in the diary indicates that he traveled from St. Louis to St. Joseph on the *Timour,* a steamboat that made regular runs between the two towns. Since the only trip of the *Timour* that fits other references began in St. Louis on 3 May, it can be assumed that Hugh Heiskell arrived in St. Louis somewhere around the first of May.

Determining to go to California might be an individual decision, but getting there overland required the cooperation of other people, and the wagon train that Hugh Heiskell joined took shape after several months of planning. The moving spirit behind the organization and the captain of the wagon train during part of the journey was Col. James W. Bicknell, a farmer and politician from Madisonville, Tennessee. Born in 1813, he grew up in Monroe County, where his father was one of the early settlers. He left the family holdings along the Tennessee River to move to Madisonville, the largest town in the county, where in partnership with his father he ran a commercial establishment. He also farmed land just outside of town. His colonelcy was very likely a courtesy title connected with his political activities, though it could have been legitimately conferred by election to the rank at the annual militia muster. He became postmaster of Madisonville in 1836 and continued in the office until 1842. He married Elizabeth King Heiskell, daughter of a prominent landholder near Madisonville, and in the course of time they had two daughters, Elizabeth and Margaret.

In 1847 Bicknell joined Company C of the Fifth Tennessee Volunteer Infantry Regiment as a private, but he saw no active combat in Mexico. His service in the army of occupation was brief, and he received a medical discharge in Mexico in February 1848.[8] Shortly after his return home his wife died, leaving him a widower with two small daughters. Their maternal aunt, Rachel Heiskell Tipton (Mrs. Quincy Adams Tipton), took over their care.

During the spring and summer of 1848, the news of the discovery of gold in California began to reach the general public. For people in Monroe County, the idea of panning gold out of creeks and rivers was in no way remarkable, for they lived near enough to be well acquainted with the gold mining that took place across the county border in North Carolina and in the adjacent Cherokee country in northern Georgia. Letters in 1830–31 to and from William M. Stakely, a merchant in Madisonville, indicate that he and at least some of his customers were familiar with the mining methods used in the Georgia field, and even with basic gold-assaying techniques.[9] Presumably, the same would have been true for his fellow merchant, Bicknell.

James W. Bicknell apparently decided to seek a new life in California, making the journey overland to the gold fields. He gathered about him a group of young men, most of them recent college graduates or young professionals. Joining him were his brother-in-law, Tyler Davis Heiskell, not long out of Emory and Henry College, and Tyler's cousin from Knox County, Hugh Brown Heiskell, who was about to embark on a career as a lawyer. Another Monroe Countian was Dr. Oliver P. White, who had just completed his medical studies at Transylvania University in Kentucky.[10] His decision to make the trip to California may well have been influenced by the fact that there were already five doctors practicing in the town of Madisonville, which had only four hundred inhabitants. Setting up a practice there would have brought him into rivalry with, among others, Dr. William Bicknell, who had finished his course of study at Transylvania only a year or two earlier. For Dr. White, the professional possibilities in a rapidly growing new territory could have added to the lures of gold and adventure. Richard L. White (the doctor's brother), Nelson Cannon, Anderson Humphreys, John Brown, and Cornelius Howard, all from Monroe County, rounded out the group.

Bicknell also was in touch with Donald Campbell, who had moved from Tennessee to Alabama and was farming land near Florence in that state. Campbell put together a party who would join the Monroe Countians: himself, Alex, John, and Alph Campbell; a black teenage slave also named Alex; some other young white men; two young free blacks; and a "Major" Bassett. Since another resident of the Florence area named Griffith appears later as the driver of a wagon, the large Campbell party may have divided into two groups as the train was finally made up.

For East Tennesseans who intended to go to California, the fastest and most convenient method of travel to the jumping off points in Missouri was by water. Some venturesome ones, like Clayton and Robert Reeve and their sister Rebecca, took advantage of the spring rains and sailed a homemade flatboat down the Tennessee River, hiring a pilot to get them over the worst rapids. After thirty-two days they arrived at Paducah, Kentucky, caught a steamboat to St. Louis, and then another up the Missouri to Independence, where they arrived 24 April.[11]

More typical, perhaps, was John Evans Brown of Asheville, North Carolina, who left a daily journal of his trip across the mountains to Knoxville to take a steamboat to St. Louis.

All day Wednesday [21 March 1849] we remained in Knoxville endeavoring to sell the waggon and horses, finally succeeding in disposing of Roberts' horse, the Company remaining in the house fiddling away the time. On Thursday we divided in shares our equipment, my share being a horse, bridle and saddle, which I immediately sold for Fifty Dollars. I then went on board of boat, "Sam Martin." I formed a mess with Haines, Mason and Atkinson, of Jonesboro, East Tennessee. There are other young men on board bound for California. One Hundred and Nine miles from home.

March 23rd. Friday. Our boat has been running down stream at the rate of fifteen miles an hour. The country is beautiful,—not as level as I had anticipated, only small flat pieces of land along the shore. The boat is quite crowded, chiefly men with the gold fever.

Arrived in Chattanooga early Saturday morning and went on shore in hopes of seeing Thomas Durin, but was disappointed. While the steamer is loading, many passengers walk into town to stretch their legs and are hurried back by the steamer's whistle, signalling her intention to leave the wharf. We made a fine run but "Cassindra" outstripped us.

On Sunday morning we arrived at Whitesburg, and I was agreeably surprised to find my friend, Thomas Durin, where he was preparing to leave for home. With much regret, I bade him farewell and I could not but shed a tear as he was the last of the family I would see. How many thousands of miles I shall travel before seeing those dear faces again.

We reached Decatur having made a steady run of fifteen miles an hour. We were there compelled to take cars on railroad drawn by horses. Some

Companies have their horses on board, so they go with them. After much dickering and confusion, we leave Decatur and travel at the rate of six miles an hour. The railroad is very slow after the drifting of the steamboat. We arrived at Tuscumbia, a beautiful place. It has many advantages of making a large business city. We put up for the night at the Franklin House. The Landlord is accommodating. We spend Tuesday in Tuscumbia, awaiting the arrival of a boat to carry us to the mouth of Tennessee River. The boat does not come until three o'clock Wednesday. On Thursday, we left on the steamboat, "Courtland," a beautiful boat equal in size and accommodation to any eastern boat. The officers are very gentlemanly, and the fare is as good as any I ever knew on board a boat. The landing is one of the most picturesque places I ever saw and the immense warehouse is not surpassed by anything in the world. It is built on the point of hill and is a very durable building. I lost Ten Dollars in gold this evening.

March 30th. Friday. Made but little distance at first, owing to the great quantity of cotton on board. There was much gambling onboard. The country through which we passed was very fine, but unimproved. The rich river bottoms are much neglected, perhaps because of their liability to overflow, the banks being quite low.

Saturday, we gently sail on. March went out very pleasantly indeed. With but four exceptions we have had fine weather to travel in. The boat took in two hundred tons of pig metal from the furnace of Stackal. I walked about two miles to the place, and was surprised to find the richest kind of fossil ore, and quite convenient. This makes a very fine metal.

Sunday, April 1st. A beautiful day, but a little cold, fires being quite comfortable. We were running at the rate of fifteen miles an hour, while the water was nearly over the guard. Reaching Paducah as a boat from Cincinnati was coming in, I immediately, on her landing, engaged passage for all of our men, Ne Plus Ultra, at $3.50 to St. Louis. There are nearly one hundred and fifty persons from Boston on board, who are bound for California.

The next morning we awoke to find ourselves at the wharf in St. Louis.[12]

Just three weeks later, the Bicknell party made the same journey. Two different members wrote of leaving "home" on 16 April, but they did not specify the point of departure, although Hugh Heiskell's niece identified it as Knoxville. Only shallow draft vessels could travel the upper Tennessee, but the *Cassandra,* George Nicholson, master, was one of three steamboats at Knoxville that regularly made connections with the lower Tennessee packet boats operating out of Florence and Tuscumbia, Alabama. The *Cassandra* left Knoxville on 16 April for Decatur, Alabama, where a brief overland trip past the rapids (Mussel Shoals) took travelers to Florence. There Hugh Heiskell and the Monroe Countians could have joined with their fellow travelers, Donald Campbell and his group, to catch the lower river packet, which left on Saturday and made connections that would have landed them in St. Louis by the first of the month.[13]

In the spring of 1849 a cholera epidemic swept up the Mississippi from New Orleans, hitting St. Louis just as the full tide of California emigrants reached the city. Many travelers never got beyond St. Louis, and others carried the infection up the Missouri to Independence, St. Joseph, and out on to the plains. The Quaker forty-niner Charles Pancoast speaks of some sixty deaths aboard the vessel on which he was a passenger out of St. Louis. Both crew and passengers abandoned the *Monroe,* on which some fifty-three fatalities occurred on the trip upriver. The town authorities at St. Joseph, learning that the *Mary* had numerous cholera cases on board, refused to permit their landing, and the captain had to discharge his passengers into the unsettled area across the river.[14]

The *Timour,* under the command of Capt. William Miller, was a new vessel launched in March at St. Louis and designed for the Missouri River trade. Originally scheduled to leave for St. Joseph on 2 May, she was delayed until the third of the month by some unnamed difficulty. Once started, however, she made good time, meeting the *Algoma* at Grimes Landing on the fifth and reaching St. Joseph on the ninth. The *Timour* had only one case of cholera, a member of the crew.[15]

Since the first portion of Hugh Heiskell's diary is missing, the journey from St. Louis to St. Joseph and the beginning of the long trek across the plains can be followed only through a series of letters he wrote to his family in May, June, and July, giving details of their buying oxen, wagons, and supplies in St. Joseph; their move across the river into the open prairie; and incidents on the way to Fort Laramie.[16]

[St. Joseph, Missouri
17 May 1849]

Dear Father—We have now tried camp-life one week, and enjoy it finely. Though we have had a great deal of rain and wind, we have been as busy in our tents as we would have been in a house. With a buffalo rug for our bed, we are much more comfortable than many are in their more costly dwellings. Our domicil is nine feet square and nine feet high, the sides being four feet high before the slope begins.

Everything necessary for an out-fit to California is exhorbitantly high at St. Joseph. Mules of suitable age are not to be had at any price, Government having purchased a great many last Fall; and what were left had been taken by emigrants who reached here before we did. Those of two or three years of age are plenty at from seventy-five to a hundred dollars, but such are considered to be too young to endure the journey.

We have concluded to make the trip with oxen; and they, too, are very high—fifty to eighty-five dollars a yoke. . . . The Col. Tyler and myself have purchased four yoke at an average of sixty-two and a half dollars. . . . The other mess, Brown, Humphreys, Halvard [Howard, as corrected in later note], and the two Whites, have four yoke, a very fine team.—We also have purchased a hardy little horse at fifty dollars, and a three-year-old mule at eighty.

To-morrow we go to the plains, eight miles off, where grass is plenty.

Saturday, 19th—Yesterday we reached the plains, and on the 21st (Monday), we take up the line of march for California. Mr. Campbell [Donald Campbell of Florence, Alabama], will move out to-day. With him are six young men, and his black boy; an old gentleman, Mr. Bassett, and two free Negro boys. We also have with us Capt. Dent's company, consisting of five, including the Captain's servant, with three wagons. Capt. Dent is the son of a rich farmer near St. Louis, and commanded a company in Mexico, is much of a gentleman, free, open-hearted, will risk his life to serve a friend, and withal, is most energetic and thorough-going. Other small parties we have seen will wait for us at the *mission,* twenty miles ahead, where we will organize a company of about fifty, with Capt. Tiplin [Taplin], who was with Col. Fremont in his last expedition, as our guide. Thus manned and equip, we set out on a trip that may test, in more ways than one, the materials of which we are made.

Our Monroe mess are determined not to travel on the Sabbath, and as this is Mr. Campbell's feeling, it will no doubt be confirmed by the whole company, particularly as there will be with us a Methodist preacher who has regular morning and evening prayers. Up to this time I have witnessed nothing like disorder or immorality—all read their Bibles and demean themselves with the utmost propriety. T—— improves rapidly. A Sabbath or two ago, he read several chapters in his Bible and seven prayers in Hannah Moore's Private devotion, which he thought would last him until the next Sunday.[17]

Last week about eight hundred emigrants were at St. Joseph, and notwithstanding this large number, thrown together from every quarter, armed to the teeth, or as the boatsman would have it, 'loaded with arms to the guards', with all the confusion incident to purchasing their out-fit, and crossing the river with some two hundred wagons, all demeaned themselves in an orderly and genteel manner.

The cholera is prevailing to a considerable extent along the river; but so far we have escaped, and as we are now in a healthy region, we cherish the hope that Providence will still protect and preserve us, and that this fearful scourge will not overtake us. Tyle, Humphreys, and D. White were some little unwell, but all are now rejoicing in good health.

Our wagon-cover, which cost eighteen and a half dollars, is made of sail-cloth, and is so fixed that we can set the wagon bed in it, by which means we have a light boat for crossing water-courses.

We paid from five to six cents for bacon; and for flour, put up in sacks, covered with skins, we paid $6.66 per hundred, tho' at the mills it may be had at three or four dollars a barrel. But it ought to be generally known that at St. Joseph emigrants for California are most shamefully imposed upon. They are required to pay exhorbitant prices for all they need. This being the last point at which any thing can be procured for the trip, they are

. . . .
"Camp at St. Joseph," drawing by J. Goldsborough Bruff, 1849. Reproduced by permission of the Huntington Library, San Marino, California.

A Forty-niner from Tennessee

obliged to give whatever is asked, and that is high enough, in all conscience
. . . . It will be well for all who may hereafter travel this route to be sure to
buy every thing they need before moving higher up than St. Louis.

Many who have started for California, either lacking the nerve, or the
novelty having worn off, have abandoned the enterprise in despair. Every
day last week, a wagon or two, with the out-fit, was sold out by persons who
had determined to return.

I enclose a bill of our out-fit, which may be considered a pretty full one
for three persons.

Your son,

[Hu B. Heiskell][18]

Three days later, Hugh Heiskell wrote to his younger sister Sue from the camp
they had set up on the prairie across the river from St. Joseph, where they were
perfecting their organization for the first leg of the trip.

Dear Sus

We are encamped by the side of a beautiful little branch clear & pure,
which is refreshing after being confined a week or two to the muddy waters of the Missouri. This stream winds its crooked course through richer
lands than you ever saw. This Prarie country is very pretty, here it is rolling, hilly as our own East Tennessee farm, but covered with grass, which at
a distance resembles a wheat field. Along the branches & in the damp hol-
lows are clusters of trees giving shading to the green landscape. Interspersed
at pleasing intervals are Sweet William, light & deep pink, a beautiful blue
flower found with us but not common. Coral thru pastel, blue and of a
dimune rounded form (excuse my unbotanical expressions). Several other
kinds. The variety not great but the flowers are rich. Good night.

Monday 21. That beautiful clear stream spoken of last night is this morning muddy and black as tar water. The rain yesterday raised it some five feet.
It commenced rising at dark last night, and this morning by 6 o clock has
fallen 3 feet. But a spring branch puts into it which running over a rocky
bed is clear this morning.

We are now out of the States and start tomorrow across the boundless
Prairie twelve hundred [miles] to the South Pass about 600 miles to Fort

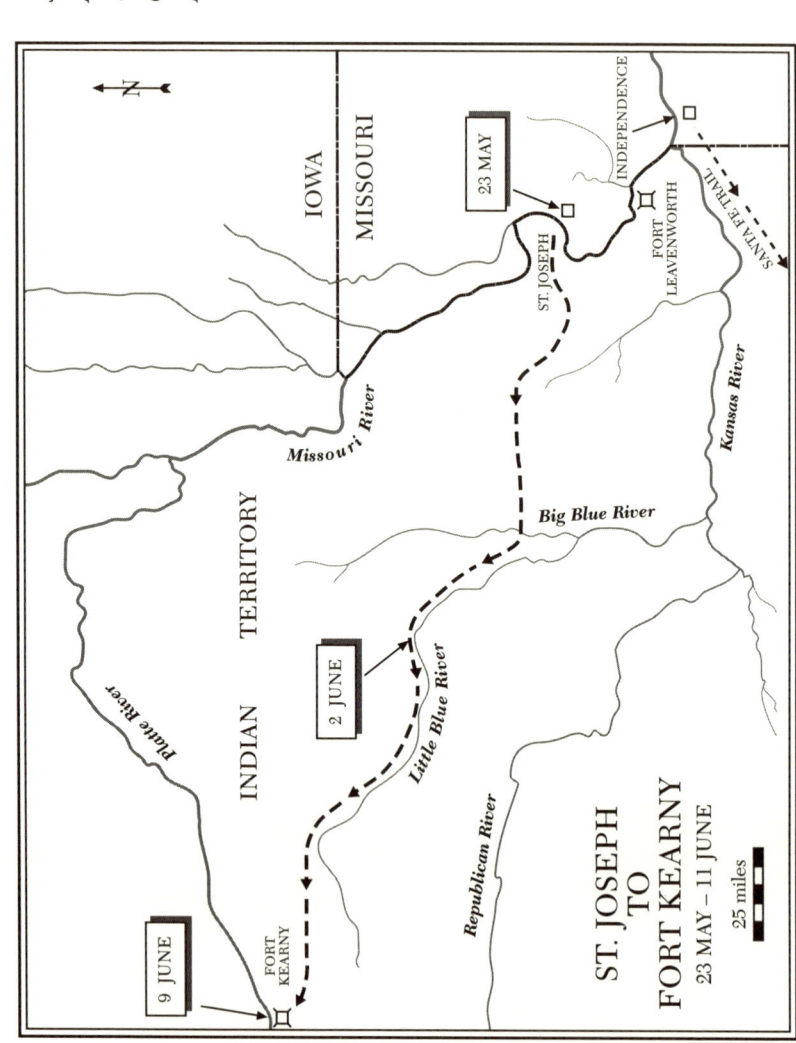

St. Joseph to Fort Kearny.
Map courtesy of the
University of Tennessee
Cartographic Services
Laboratory.

Larimie. I will try to write again from there. Here are now thousands & thousands of acres of cleared land, in grass, richer land than our bottoms. A fine country for grass. A man might have cattle upon a thousand hills here. The countless million that might [be] pastured can not be told.

It is one of the wonders of the world, one of the misteries of nature. What has caused these Prairies, it would seem as if some populous nation, had thickly inhabited this country once,—all traces of which had passed away,—That they had cleared these lands all up, or left clumps of trees here & there for shade to their cattle. And that the grass had been burnt off ever since by the Indians. Sprouts put up vigorously every year in the Prairie but the fire of the succeeding year kills them. The sprouts & trees in damp places are of course not so much effected.

Many families are on their way to California. Some little children & young ladies. But Sus as much as I love you & would like to see you I would rather you would be at home than here.

I take much pleasure Sus in in [*sic*] fancying you, an accomplished girl—when I come home—in the important branches of a good education such as Arithmetic chemistry Botany etc. & in music & singing. [Susan may have been attending the East Tennessee Female Institute, which awarded its graduates the degree of Mistress of Polite Literature.]

But Sus the important matter is to cultivate the heart. & above all be cheerful. You have no care, but everything to make you thankful then rejoice & be glad & lighthearted. It is like everything else, just as you habituate yourself now so you will live.

Read some every day, but don't forget to "bound like Roebucks o'er the plain."

Good bye Dear Sus, you will hear from me at Fort Larimie.

Your brother

H. B. Heiskell[19]

No letter from Laramie appears among the correspondence that Susan Heiskell preserved, but her niece transcribed two other letters written along the way to Fort Laramie that give details of the life of their wagon train. The first, to his sister Margaret, was written on a Sunday three weeks into the trip.

Dear Mag—

We are resting today—Sunday—in sight of Fort Kearney, near enough to hear the morning reviele [*sic*], altho one mile and a half away—If you could see me <u>now</u> with my best <u>summer</u> boots, nicely blacked. (I blacked yesterday evening week, and it was too cool, Sunday, to wear them)—with a clean hickory shirt—a <u>satin</u> vest, Jeans coat & pants, and myself clean-shaved, You would call me tolerably genteel, & I don't know but you might kiss me. The <u>shaving</u>, Mag, was done <u>this morning</u>. It would have been done last night—but we drove 20 miles, got here late, and was busy until bed-time, getting wood—which I carried 3/4 of a mile, on Betty—the mule—pitching tents—cooking supper, tying up oxen, &c, &c.

But I look upon it, as sort of a religious act—to be clean on Sunday, "the Sabbath was made for man, not man for the Sabbath." Don't make that, Mag, a cloak for what you wish to do Sunday, & I will try not. We are de-termined, to <u>not</u> travel on Sunday, unless some times we are compelled to do so, in order to get wood & water. We rest, altho many things are done, which would not look right at Fruit Hill—for instance, wood is cut, al-though, if near we cut it Saturday evening; cooking—and sometimes sun-ning whatever may be damp in the wagon. Some in the company have washed. Our mess of nine will not. Tyle says he will wash Saturday night, first.

We have <u>nine</u>, just the <u>right sort of fellows</u>. We live like brothers and would each & every one of us—stand by any other one until the last; in any difficulty no one would inquire, "is he right"—but help him out. We stick so close together that in any company matter we always stick to-gether—and thus have more influence than any other party in the company. The whole company get along amicably—as well as men thrown together can—but <u>we</u>, as brothers.

You were, and are yet, I expect, at a loss to find St. Jo—and the route we are travelling. St. Jo is in Buchanan County—116 miles above Indepen-dence—and 67 miles above Ft. Leavenworth. It has not been in existence more than five or six <u>years</u>, and is not laid down in the maps.

Get Frémont's Map—Father borrowed it from the gentleman who pur-chased Mr Bell's farm. You will find that Mitchell, in his map, makes the Missouri enter the State at its juncture with the Kansas River, whereas Ft

Leavenworth 40 or 50 miles above is in the State—and St. Jo—still higher up on the East bank—is in Missouri. The <u>West bank</u> is Indian Territory. The fact is the Missouri runs along the line at St. Jo—and some miles below—and then enters the State.

But—Tyle is calling me to dinner—a welcome call at any time, you know, and one I seldom fail to obey. Fashionable dinner today—4 oclock.

I have dined sumpt[u]ously—now let me give you our dinner and then we will go on with our travel. In the first place, yesterday evening, Mr. Taplin (our guide) went to the Fort, and came back with a nice quarter, and divided it out among the company. From this—we had most excellent soup. Soup you know is a <u>city-dish</u>, very common for dinner—but <u>with us, a luxury.</u>

Well! with a Buffalo-rug spread upon the <u>grass to keep it out of the dishes, our nine men,</u> seated around—and Mr. Taplin, Captain Dent & Mr Campbell, who came to take a <u>bowl</u> of soup with us, we fell to work— each one provided with a plate, a tin cup and big iron spoon. The soup— highly seasoned with crackers broken into it—was the <u>first</u> course. Roast beef and biscuit the <u>second</u>. Dessert came up missing. Ah! but we had that last Sunday.

Now I will give you last Sunday's dinner. I will not finish this letter but write to father.

On yesterday week Saturday Brown shot a young antelope, and we caught up with the train by 1 oclock—it is to tell you how we got the wherewithal to make <u>soup</u> the next day—we divided the antelope among the whole company. We had some fine soup at 4 oclock and roasted the piece which we had boiled, to make the soup—and a finer roast venison, nobody ever saw. Tyle made some <u>apple-pies</u> for the Sabbath dinner. What! apple pies? Yes! Mag. <u>Apple pies—twelve hundred miles from home, and 100 miles from the habitation of white men.</u>

Sunday came, and Brown made the Soup. Tyle baked biscuit—a nice ham of Venison was boiled, and soup made from the water. The ham was then taken out and roasted. Ah! and I don't want a nicer piece to grace the head of the table at Fruit Hill—at my <u>infair dinner</u>. Roast Venison and biscuits, light with saleratus, we make no other sort. We were not particular about the "courses" but mixed them to suit ourselves—3rd course, or Dessert—

dried apple pie. Mr. Taplin dined with us, as today, and we are always glad to have him.

Now to go on—where we left off—if you remember I can find the place.

With Frémont's map before you, if you cannot find Buchanan county on Mitchell's—pass your finger a little above Fort Leavenworth to thirty nine degrees and thirty nine minutes—and you will be near our starting point—our course lying nearly parallel to the Big Nimshaw—We came into the Independence road—130 miles from St. Jo—you will see it lies up the Kansas. Independence is cut off of Frémont's map, it is below the mouth of the Kansas, and four miles from the Missouri—Going on—35 miles from where we got into the Independence Road, we came to the little Blue, Saturday (yesterday week) where we had the <u>venison</u> I said Brown, the Colonel & myself—rode up it in the morning—the road was in <u>half a mile of it, in the morning</u> but we did not strike it until evening. All traders call this the Republican Fork and so does our Company, but I follow Frémont—you see the Republican Fork farther South, both emptying into the Kansas. We traveled 40 miles up the Blue—then left it—in six miles we came to a branch of the Blue—not running now—but there is a Lagoon of standing water with which we filled our casks and drove 8 miles to camp. We had a pond for the cattle to drink out of—and the water in the casks for ourselves, and yesterday we came 20 miles to Fort Kearney—situated opposite Big or Grand Island—making 170? miles to St. Jo—which I find to be so since I finished mother's letter.

In mother's letter, I put a flower for Susan Heiskell. I send you a red flower and a purple one which last is the same I think as the flower Frémont calls "Amorphia"—Page 16 of his "Expedition for 1842-3-4." I had a beautiful rose pressed for you—but it has dropped out of the book.

But my sheet is full and no place to sign my name.
Your brother
—H. B. Heiskell.[20]

Three weeks later, Hugh Heiskell wrote his father, giving more details of the organization of the company and their daily life.

Dear Father
We are resting today—Sabbath—at "Camp Ann," which I named for

Ann and the Company have so entered it on their journal. It is this side of Ft. Laremie 145 miles and 527 miles from Independence. There is here a pretty little spring—quite cool water trickling down from the side of a ridge—which runs parallel to the river. The spring is quite a luxury and although [the letter is burned here].

Last Monday we came where Buffalo were plenty. Taplin (our guide) came in at noon—his horse loaded with beef—having killed two large Buffalo Bulls. After dinner a party consisting of Taplin, Col. Bicknell, Dr. White and I went out to bring in the remainder. We had not gone more than 3 miles, when we descried <u>eight or ten</u> Buffalo quietly feeding—some two miles distant. The Colonel and Dr. White started after them to try and kill one—the rest of us going on for what was <u>already killed</u>.

Seeing an antelope, I tried to get a shot but failing, and not coming up with Campbell and Taplin easily—I went toward where Dr. White and the colonel were slipping up on the Buffalo—seeing them—& the Buffalo—moving off, I put spurs to my horse and turned round to head them in rising a slope [the letter is burned].

Remember we were among the Platte hills—without trees, covered with grass—sometimes Tableland for miles—but generally rolling with many valley & gorges.

About <u>300</u> yards off were <u>13</u> large Buffalo Bulls. Trying to slip up on them & finding I could not, I mounted my horse for a race, the Buffalo, by this time about a half a mile ahead. I put forth the utmost speed—for about 3 miles—In the meantime three New Yorkers[21] joined the race—they were out hunting [the letter is burned].

To kill Buffalo all that is wanted is a good horse, rifle & pistol, and one expert and skillful hunter can kill enough to supply 500 men. But it is death on horses. Our three days hunting have almost used ours up. With the care taken of them since, they have gotten over it. A great many horses are lost in hunting. If your horse stumbles and gets you off, he is gone—or if when you shoot you let him get away—there being no limbs to tie to—it is hard to secure him—he joins the band of Buffalo and you lose him. I lost a coat and holster-pistol when mine ran away—the coat dropped off. We have heard of half a dozen or so horses lost.

Mr. Campbell is unfortunate. Soon after shooting he left his mule, having picketed it out one night—the next morning it was gone. Next, he broke

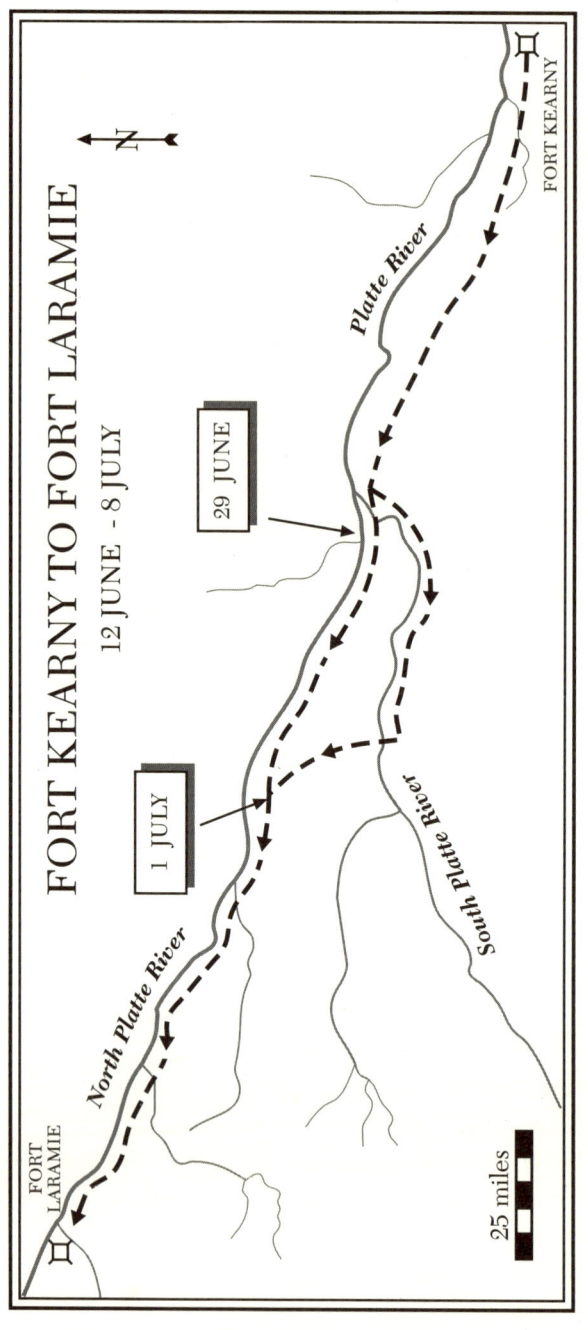

Fort Kearny to Fort Laramie. Map courtesy of the University of Tennessee Cartographic Services Laboratory.

his wagon—got another at Ft. Kearney and now he has lost <u>Carle's horse</u>. I must give you an account of our camping—as from my letter dated from Missouri [the letter is burned].

<u>We try to average 16 miles a day, sometimes we travel 20</u>. Yesterday & day before we traveled 22 & 21 miles in order to get to water. When we stop for the night, the wagons are driven one behind the other, and the tents are pitched parallel with the wagons—with a space of 20 feet between to give room for cooking, &c, &c— The cattle are turned out to graze, and the horses are turned loose or picketed, according to whether they are wild or not. The cattle are tied up at night, and the horses picketed behind the tents so as to be in sight of the guard, who walks between the tents and wagons, and around the horses. Three persons stand guard during the night. The first watch standing until 12 oclock—the Second from 12 until 2 A.M.— the third from 2 [the letter is burned]. Two persons are appointed—alphabetically—to guard the cattle, during the day, to keep them from scattering off—and to drive them up and water them. We have <u>Seventy-three head of cattle, four</u> of them are milk cows. Our company consists of about 39 persons. There are 4 black boys. [The letter is burned.] A Mr. Thomas & wife—a singular man from England, with a very clever wife. With him are a Scotchman & a Dutchman. Carle, from the Highlands—an intelligent & honest specimen of the true Scotch. A Dr. Brown, with four other men from St. Louis. Brown is a young man from Bavaria—is well educated and understands several languages [the letter is burned].

If the Rail-Road ever comes here, or thro' here, timber will have to be transported from the states, as there is none here—except Cottonwood— which is fit for nothing. [The letter is burned.]
Hu B. Heiskell[22]

People crossing the plains in 1849 usually organized themselves into mess units, frequently identified with one wagon. The Bicknell train consisted of some nine or ten messes and originally twelve wagons. Some messes and companies were organized under elaborate written rules and bylaws, while others depended only on oral agreements. No evidence exists to show that Hugh Heiskell's group agreed to written rules.[23]

The identity of the first mess and wagons of the Bicknell company can be asserted with some certainty, but the information about the others is fragmentary. In mess number one were James W. Bicknell, Hugh Brown Heiskell, Tyler Davis Heiskell, Dr. O. P. White, Richard L. White, John Brown, Cornelius Howard, Nelson Cannon, and Anderson Humphreys, the Monroe County contingent who traveled in two wagons.

It is presumed that mess number two was headed by Charles Taplin, whom they had been fortunate enough to secure as their guide. Taplin led an adventurous life. In 1842 he signed on as a voyageur in John C. Frémont's second expedition and joined him in the third expedition. At the request of Jessie Benton Frémont, President James K. Polk commissioned Taplin as a first lieutenant in the army, and he left the explorer's employment just before the formation of the California battalion. He may have served unofficially as an aide in that unit, but his name does not appear in the few battalion records that have survived. With Joseph Walker and others he drove a large herd of horses from southern California to Fort Hall, where with two companions he proceeded to Fort Leavenworth to join the 12th Infantry Regiment. In the battles of Contreras and Churubusco he was cited for meritorious conduct and was later promoted to brevet captain, but he resigned from the army after Frémont's court-martial. He then joined Frémont's disastrous fourth expedition and barely survived the attempt to cross the mountains in winter, but three months after the rescue party reached them, he recovered sufficiently to accept the job of guiding Hugh Heiskell's company. Later, he served as wagon master of the Gunnison expedition and as field geologist for Capt. John Pope's exploration of a railroad route across Texas. One forty-niner who overtook the Bicknell train along the way has left a description of Taplin:

> The guide was a man of about 40 bronzed & hardy looking, but neatly dressed in frontier costume & intelligent in his conversation. He had a long & very handsome rifle which showed evident signs of much & hard usage, a revolver with Bowie Knife & hatchet stuck in his belt & Mexican spurs some three inches in length, completed his attire. His horse was one of the hardy mustangs & he had a Mexican saddle, high fore & aft with large wooden stirrups nearly large enough to cover the entire foot. He was altogether quite an object of interest to me as I have almost as great respect for Frémont as had he.[24]

Perkins's group, a mule train, left St. Joseph nearly a week after the Bicknell party, overtook them on 8 June near the Little Blue River, about two-thirds of the way to Fort Kearny, camped with them on the Little Blue over the Sunday, and moved on ahead on the eleventh.

The contingent from Alabama made up the next group, more than half of whose names are uncertain. Donald Campbell headed the mess. In his diary, Hugh Heiskell also mentions a son, Alex; a teenager, John Campbell; an Alph Campbell (perhaps another son); and a young black slave named Alex. In addition there was a Mr./Major Bassett, four young white men, and two young free men of color.

Next came a three-wagon group, that of Captain Dent, who abandoned one wagon just beyond Green River. There were four other people in his party, including one servant. John Dent, son of a Missouri planter, rose from second lieutenant to captain, commanding Company B, 2d Regiment of Missouri Volunteers in the Mexican War. He participated in one major engagement but spent most of his time with the disgruntled soldiers assigned to garrison duty in Santa Fe while other units were sent on to California. Later in life he achieved some prominence in Washington during the presidential administration of his brother-in-law, Ulysses S. Grant. All of these men assembled on the plains across from St. Joseph in the third week in May.[25]

Colonel Bicknell's group completed their organization at the mission, some fifty miles west of St. Joseph. Wagon number seven and its mess consisted of "Judge" Barnes, his wife, daughter, and son; the diary identifies no other members of their mess. Wagon number eight and its mess contained Mr. and Mrs. Thomas, who were of English birth; a "Dutch" driver named Frank; and a Scottish Highlander named Carle. Doctor Thompson, who had an adolescent slave named Wash, commanded wagon number nine. Griffith, who like Campbell was a former resident of Alabama, had a wagon and mess of his own. The diarist names two other men, Cockerill and Dr. Brown, as heads of messes. Brown was from St. Louis, as were other members of his group. Since Hugh Heiskell mentions only the abandonment of Dent's wagon at Taplin Creek, the train may have lost the other wagon of the original twelve before reaching Green River.[26]

As finally organized, the Bicknell train consisted of twelve wagons and about fifty people. The train is known to have included three women, Mrs. Barnes, her unnamed daughter, and Mrs. Thomas.[27] At least four blacks were a part of the train: Alex and Wash, slaves belonging respectively to Donald Campbell and Dr.

Thompson, and two unnamed free blacks; in a letter, the diarist refers to a servant of Captain Dent, but whether he was black or a slave is not known.[28] Allowing four or six oxen to each wagon, plus known riding horses and spare animals, the train would have counted some eighty-five to a hundred draft oxen, horses, and mules. The diarist mentions no formal charter of incorporation, but he does note that Colonel Bicknell on 5 September "resumed" the post of captain of the company from Captain Dent, whose term had expired, indicating that understandings had been reached earlier, either orally or on paper. Some larger groups broke up because at the end of a day's journey they had difficulty finding adequate forage for so many animals. Other groups came to a parting of ways over what route to follow, dissatisfaction with the leaders, or personal quarrels. References in later letters indicate that Bicknell's group remained together during the whole trip, though not without dissension. Hugh Heiskell records that Griffith helped Campbell during the ordeal of crossing the desert, although they had not been speaking to one another for some time because of a quarrel. Dr. O. P. White and Dr. Thompson came close to a personal encounter when Dr. White shot Thompson's unruly horse. Slavery, that pervading bone of contention in contemporary America, provoked one quarrel when Mr. Thomas, at his wife's instigation, tried to prevent Donald Campbell from punishing his slave Alex. A fistfight broke out between Dr. White and Mr. Thomas because the latter drove between the two Monroe County wagons. Besides these incidents, however, Hugh does not record major dissension within the train. The expertise of their guide, Charles Taplin, and the service of Bicknell and Captain Dent in the Mexican War may have given their group more effective leadership than many others enjoyed.[29]

The degree of discipline maintained by different groups varied a great deal, and the forty-niner migration bore little resemblance to a centrally directed army on the march. Disorder and casual interchanges were the rule. Emigrants visited back and forth between trains, shared information (and misinformation), and depended on the knowledge of others to add to the inadequate printed guidebooks that were available. Wagons might fall behind their train because of necessary repairs or lost animals, attach themselves loosely to the next passing company for the protection it afforded against Indians, and catch up with their original companions as opportunity offered. Horsemen who became impatient with the slow pace of oxen sometimes abandoned their trains and took their chances alone with a pack animal. Mule trains overtook the slower ox-drawn wagons, so that two groups might intermingle for the better part of a day. Ferries on the Platte and Green Rivers created bottlenecks and bunched up separate trains. Alternative routes sometimes brought a group out ahead of a train that formerly preceded them. Some emigrants went via Salt Lake City and benefited from the replenishment of supplies and equipment that the Mormon settlements offered; when they set out again they might find themselves a week or more behind those who had taken Sublette's Cut-off. Some trains broke up completely in the face of difficulties, as did a group of Germans who set out unprepared to cross the desert from Salt Lake City and lost all their wagons and most of their draft animals in Hastings' Cut-off. They continued on as individuals, attaching themselves to other groups and often depending on them for food. Hugh Heiskell mentions three such casual companions, identifying them with a company they had met on the Platte River.

Two of the better-known groups whose paths intertwined with Bicknell's were Bruff's train and Turner and Allen's Pioneer Line. J. Goldsborough Bruff, commander of the highly disciplined Washington City Company, kept two different journals and made numerous sketches along the way. The Bicknell and Bruff trains were only a few days apart on the trail and overlapped one another at times. In his diary entry for 9 September, Hugh Heiskell refers to something "that Bruff told us." From the few dated locations of Hugh's party during June and July, it seems likely that the Bicknell train rested for several days at Fort Kearny, making repairs and preparing for the next leg of the journey to Fort Laramie. J. Goldsborough Bruff notes that as he was approaching Fort Kearny on 16 June he passed the camps of several trains from St. Joseph. After three days spent in repairs and reorganization of his train, Bruff moved out on the nineteenth. As they were traveling up the valley of the Platte on the twenty-fifth he "supped with Capt. Brown of a Tennessee company." The two companies may have continued onward near one another as far as Fort Laramie, but beyond there Bruff's mule-drawn wagons pulled ahead of the ox companies near which he had been traveling. His diary confirms that Bruff was ahead of the Bicknell train by the time they reached the Sweetwater River and arrived at Green River some five days before them. Bruff's group maintained this five-day advantage until it took the Lassen Cut-off, while Hugh Heiskell's party passed the Lassen turn-off and continued on down the Humboldt to the Carson River trail.[30]

Two St. Louis businessmen, Allen and Turner, set up the Pioneer Line, which for a fee of $200 offered to supply food and transportation from Independence to San

Francisco, leaving in April and expecting to make the journey in sixty days. Their first train was quickly oversubscribed, and they announced a second train to leave in June. The first company met many difficulties and delays but overtook Hugh Heiskell's party as they were traveling the last hundred miles to Fort Kearny. Bernard J. Reid noted in his diary entry for Tuesday, 5 June, that he had passed three ox trains, and the Pioneer party arrived at Fort Kearny on the eighth, while the Bicknell train came in on Saturday evening, the ninth. Both Pioneer Line trains ran into major problems. The first, led by Turner, virtually disintegrated before a remnant reached California five months later; the second, led by Allen, survived its difficulties better, though by Hugh Heiskell's reckoning it had already lost one-third of its passengers when it crossed the path of the Bicknell train early in September.[31]

The journal that Hugh Heiskell kept speaks for itself as a straightforward narration and description of his adventure, but it also contains references to race, class, gender, and especially the environment, subjects that in recent years have attracted the attention of historians of the West. It differs from most other forty-niner journals in the length of the entries, for each day on the average takes up a full page in a bookkeeping ledger, while many diarists were content merely to list date, weather, mileage, and perhaps a brief comment. Each of Hugh Heiskell's entries begins with the date and the miles covered that day. He then goes into the weather and travel conditions and records the noon halt ("nooned") for food and rest. The afternoon's travel comes next and usually a description of the camping area for the night. Finally, he frequently adds other events of the day he considers noteworthy and sometimes refers to the evening activities around the campfire. One does not ordinarily think of forty-niners at the end of the day's journey discussing the life and poetry of Lord Byron or the religious preferences of Charles II, as recorded in this diary. Charles Taplin, their guide, related some of his experiences on John Charles Frémont's expeditions. Since he had actually traveled the length and breadth of California in company with Frémont or on his own, he could supply from personal observation details about the new territory that were not available to many emigrants.

Only in imagination can the original journey of the forty-niners be relived. Even if their equipment were duplicated, the path westward has become impassable for various reasons: it has been built over, it traverses private property, or it lies beneath the waters of reservoirs. A number of highways parallel the course of the wagons, but frequently at a distance that requires excursions of several miles over back roads to reach the original route; modern highway engineers, using earth-moving machines to accommodate high-speed automotive traffic have disregarded the twists and turns that the terrain imposed on the gold seekers. Farming and mining operations, highways, and dams have displaced the flora and fauna of 1849. Even areas that seem to have reverted to wilderness can be deceptive. Only a few scattered foundation stones mark the site of the once-flourishing gold camp known as Weaverville, the terminus of the Bicknell wagon train. Most of the area is covered with trees, and Webber Creek flows swift and clear under overhanging branches. A modern visitor has almost no hints that 150 years ago nearly a thousand people lived in tents and hastily built cabins that straggled along the stream. The scrub trees and briars of the present are a far cry from the forest that the early settlers encountered. To recapture in imagination the overland journey of 1849, a modern traveler needs the notes of an articulate observer like Hugh Heiskell while being mindful of the many manmade and natural changes of the past century and a half.[32]

In *Wilderness and the American Mind,* Roderick Nash focuses on the artists and writers of Hugh Heiskell's era whose works were changing the concept of "wilderness," but he omits a more pervasive influence: the educational system that was increasingly turning the American mind to a scientific view of the world. The standard curriculum in colleges required a course in natural philosophy, where students learned that the apparent chaos of nature was merely part of a universe whose basic order was indicated in the classifications of the naturalist Linnaeus or the geologist Lyell. Educated people like Hugh Heiskell and some of his companions might encounter new species or genera or strange rocks, but they already had an intellectual framework into which they could fit their experiences. In some respects, the "wilderness" they met was already "destroyed." Of course, they still retained some old concepts. Hugh Heiskell could glory in the wonder of the night skies without invoking astronomy, but when he looked at the grass in a new camping site he was interested in its scientific name and habitat and—very practically—whether it was good forage for the oxen.

True to his rural upbringing, Hugh Heiskell saw the country he traversed first of all through the eyes of a farmer, mentioning specifically the suitability of land for familiar crops, but he also looked at his surroundings with the eye of a naturalist. His own special interests furnish most of the topics of his diary: the flora and, to a lesser extent, the fauna; the scenery; the terrain; and the geological formations. In his botanical observations he frequently used scientific nomenclature

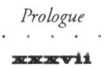

as well as common names. There are three places in the diary where specimens of plants were pressed and pasted to the pages. On a loose leaf that was glued in next to one of these are the words: "The flowers in the books were culled & pressed by Hugh during our long & toilsome journey crossing the plains." Then follows a signature of initials, "TDH." Only fragments of these plants remain, and Tyler D. Heiskell's appended note hints that other specimens may have been kept in a separate book.

Hugh Heiskell commented frequently on the Indians he met along the way. It is unlikely that as he was growing up he had had more than a passing acquaintance with Indians, if that, for Knoxville was a bustling town a generation past its frontier days. During his boyhood, the Cherokees who had dominated the area were forcibly removed to areas west of the Mississippi. He characterized the western Indians in various ways: unwanted visitors, persistent traders, horse and cattle thieves, and dangerous night raiders, but also as willing workers who helped them cut hay for the cattle before crossing the desert, finders of lost oxen, guides, and suppliers of berries, fish, and game. He described a few individuals but seems to have been interested mainly in the material culture of various tribes, comparing the tepees of the Snakes unfavorably with those of the Sioux, describing the willow beehive shelters constructed by the Paiutes, and examining in detail the neat workmanship of the arrow that wounded one of his companions.

The diarist's notations on geology show some general systematic knowledge of that science, and he uses chemical terminology in describing the composition of the waters in the springs and streams he encountered, speculating on the process by which accretions of chemical compounds produced strange formations at the hot springs, for instance. A college course in natural history and philosophy would have given him the framework for the kinds of comments that he made, which his own particular interests filled out.

This diary is noteworthy also for enlarging Sarah Bayliss Royce's classic account of her forty-niner experiences. Sarah, her husband, her daughter, and two chance-met companions started to cross from Humboldt Sink to Carson River with insufficient forage and water and were forced to turn back ten miles into the desert. They met the Bicknell train and exchanged information. Later, the Royces caught up with Bicknell's group and they traveled together at times from the Carson River to the crest of the Sierra Nevada mountains. Hugh Heiskell consistently spells their name as "Rice," which is very likely the way they said their name, for the old pronunciation of "oi" continued in use well into the nineteenth century (many Civil War soldiers "jined" the army). For a comparison of the same incident as described by Hugh Brown Heiskell and Sarah Bayliss Royce, see the entry for 20 October.

The present owner of Hugh Heiskell's journal is Anne Heiskell Nichols Wood, who received it from a cousin, Margaret Roberts Witzmann. She inherited it from her mother, Fanny Wallace Roberts, the daughter of Margaret Heiskell Wallace, Hugh Heiskell's sister. The Wallace and Roberts families used the pages of the ledger following the diary as a scrapbook in which they noted family births, deaths, and marriages, frequently accompanied by newspaper clippings about these and other social events.

In this version of the diary, the editor, who is a descendant of Hugh Heiskell's sister Susan, has changed the original text minimally, aiming to make it more readable. A standard system replaces varied ways of recording the date in the ledger. Variant spellings of names have been eliminated. The diarist sometimes started a sentence or used a word which he then scratched out; only the words he substituted appear in this edition. His original capitalization, spelling, and punctuation show deficiencies that may be blamed partly on the poor conditions under which he had to make his entries; some lapses in each of these areas have been corrected without notice to make them conform to modern usage. However, the words and phrases all belong to the keeper of the journal. Brackets indicate other interventions by the editor, such as a reading of some questionable phrase or the insertion of a missing word. A literal transcription of the diary and a microfilm of the original journal are available at the West Virginia and Regional History Collection at West Virginia University, Morgantown. The Tennessee State Library and Archives has a different microfilm of the journal, and the Bancroft Library at the University of California has a literal transcript.

The Diary of
Hugh Brown Heiskell

· · · · ·

MONDAY, AUGUST 13, 1849.
LEFT GREEN RIVER.
TRAVELED 11 MILES.

Morning cool, water in the buckets froze slightly. Started at half past 7. The road very crooked & across large hills; traveled 8 miles & nooned on a beautiful creek—on an air line not more than 4 miles. It is about 20 feet wide & one foot & a half deep. Dent's steer Sherk was found defunct this morning, making two he has lost out of the Steamboat team, the other having died at Big Sandy.[1]

The train arrived at Green River Friday night at 11 o'clock, having made the stretch in 24 traveling hours, which is forty-five miles. Green River is a beautiful clear & very swift stream, about 60 yards wide & 3 feet deep, presenting in deep places a greenish tinge. Grass short, being eat off, & alkali covering the ground. Drove the cattle to the hills where was good bunch grass, a kind of grass that grows here in arid, parched hills among the sage in bunches, the tops of them being dry, but near the ground more fresh affording nutricious food for the cattle.

Taplin related the circumstance of Fremont's getting lost at St. John's Mountain—a spur of the Sierra Madre. It was in November of '48. Leaving the Arkansas they were striking across the head waters of the del Norte to the Compadre. Fremont & Williams were riding forward as usual. There were two gaps in the

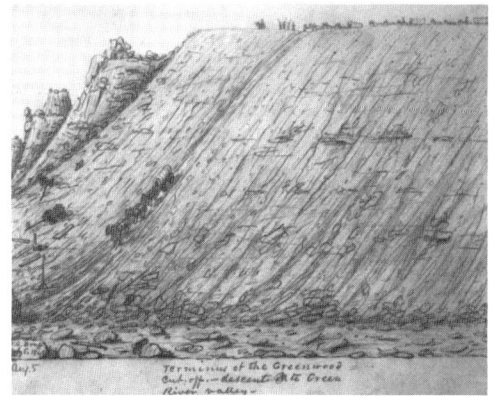

"Terminus of the Greenwood Cut-Off," drawing by J. Goldsborough Bruff, 1849. Reproduced by permission of the Huntington Library, San Marino, California.

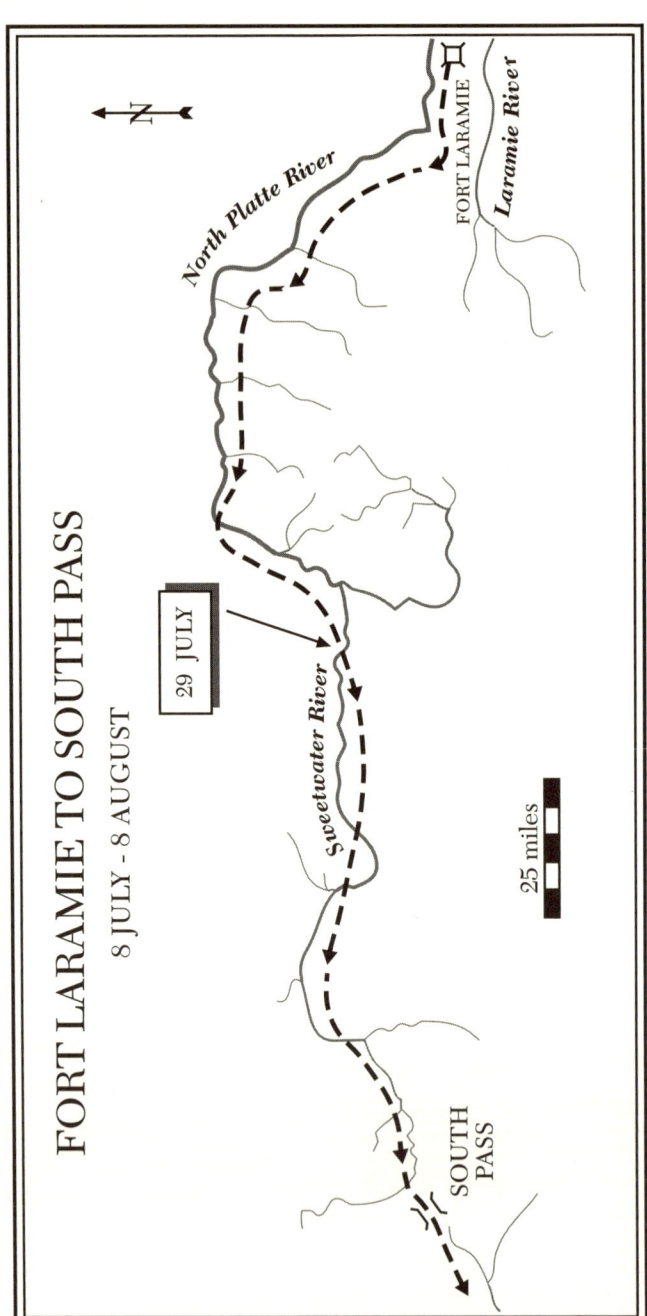

Fort Laramie to South Pass. Map courtesy of the University of Tennessee Cartographic Services Laboratory.

St. John Mountain, formed by the Del Norte & a branch farther north. In the morning they bore towards the north gap; in the evening p. m. they changed their course & bore to the southern gap. They suppose now that the northern was the right pass. Fremont says that Williams bore north in the morning, then doubting turned to the south Williams says that Fremont insisted that Williams was wrong & the Del Norte gap was the pass. Let it be between them, but Fremont being the man of influence poor Williams will have to bear the blame of misguiding & causing their disaster.

At noon the Colonel found a fine, fat cow & a large, poor steer which later we worked this evening. Moved up the creek, which we named Taplin Creek in honor of our guide, 3 miles.

. . . . .

TUESDAY, AUGUST 14, 1849.
LEFT TAPLIN CREEK.
TRAVELED 15 MILES.

Struck tents & started at half past 6, traveled ten miles, & nooned at a cool spring surrounded with small cottonwood, having past a half mile back a place where were a great many pines—Spruce—tall, shaped like Lombardy poplar. There was a spring which lost itself in a thickly brushed, swampy flat.

We lost our fine cow last evening. Just above us were some lodges of Indian traders, & Lee Anderson,[2] one of them, came down hunting a cow which proved to be the same; thus our visions of fine milk in California were dispelled.

Brown[3] & Tyle[4] rode up the creek this morning to fish & hunt. Saw some fine Trout & Tyle caught one, but seeing one of the waggons had stopt, getting uneasy they did not wait to fish long. There are some fine holes along the creek for fishing. The stream is so clear you can see the bottom where it is five or six feet deep.

The general flatness of the country is improving a little, presenting along the eastern hillsides a green appearance, the western sides the top soil or sand being blown off & settling in the western. The sage bushes are still the characteristic—which we have to use tonight to cook with. They make a quick good fire while it lasts. The water is much better—in fact as good as in any country—& has been the whole trip better than we expected. We either have a clear-running, cool mountain stream or spring at every camping place. The road this evening has been

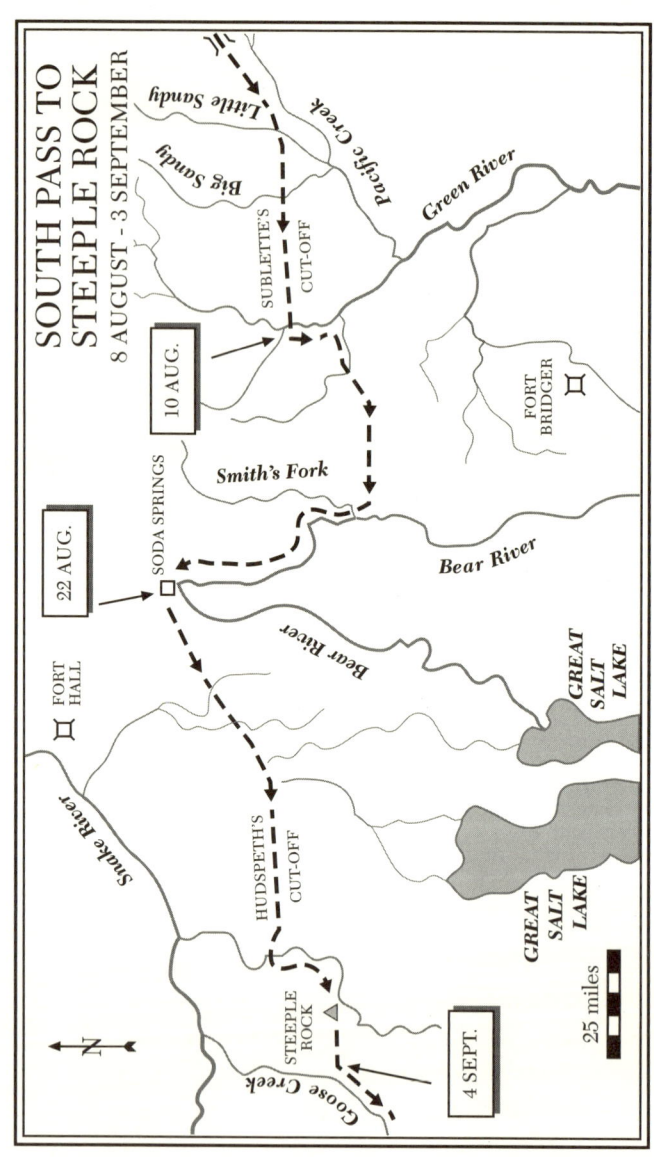

South Pass to Steeple Rock. Map courtesy of the University of Tennessee Cartographic Services Laboratory.

over steeper hills than any we have crossed. The dust as usual 3 inches deep. The wind which blows every day in our faces, blowing today slightly; covering the teamsters with dust. But it also "neutralizes" the heat of the sun—which would be oppressive at noon—making the weather pleasant.

Camped in full view of the mountain ridge that divides the waters of the Pacific from the waters of the Great Basin.

. . . . .

WEDNESDAY, AUGUST 15, 1849.
TRAVELED 17 MILES

Decamped at seven. Morning as usual cool, road through a mountainous country—though with the exception of two or three hills that we descended & the crossing of some miry branches—good & tolerably level

Traveled 7 miles & nooned to the left of the road a half of a mile, where we found most excellent grass. Made coffee, which we have got to using three times a day. Brown's mess are cleaning out their wagon & throwing away every pound's weight they think they can do without, taking care not to throw away any provisions. The whole train is in fact making every shift to lighten the wagons.[5]

On yesterday Captain Dent & Elliott[6] left the Steamboat wagon on Taplin Creek owing to their having lost 3 steers, two having died & one strayed off.

The dividing ridge running north & south to our right, the prominent points barren & bare, the intervening spaces flats & ravines green with bushes, sage, & grass. The soil improving, grass found everywhere. Among the sage there is scattered some. The grass resembles herdsgrass. It is remarked that we passed no dead cattle to day, which is encouraging, for heretofore since crossing the north fork of Platte the route might be traced by the dead cattle that are strewed every half mile along the road.

Having traveled 10 miles we camped on Ham's Fork, a clear stream 25 feet wide & two deep, with fine trout. Grass plenty & fine. Having arrived at half past 3, I took hook & line & went fishing. Commencing with the patience of Sir Isaac Walton; not getting any bites, I soon tired.

We are camped near some French traders. They have formed Indian connections, have a good many fine horses & cattle. There are a great many traders among these Indian tribes. They are principally Canadian French. Some of the company wishing to trade—they ask from one to two hundred dollars for horses; from one hundred to one twenty-five for a yoke of cattle.

Bear River Mountains in view to our left Southwest of us.

. . . . .

THURSDAY, AUGUST 16, 1849.
LEFT HAM'S FORK.
TRAVELED 16 MILES.

Heavy frost. Decamped at 7 o'clock. After traveling up the river about a mile we crossed it & the bottom 600 yards with which it is skirted, covered with Blue Bunch & Buffalo grass, the soil being rich. The river banks are lined with willow bushes. After crossing we started across the divide, a high hill, then the road until noon most excellent.

We are in the midst of the mountains. The soil, fine black mould, would bring fine wheat. Scenery very pretty. The lower tableland covered with bunch grass which presents a yellowish appearance, the tops being dry & sage with its yellow flowers—but which is not so thick set or large today as usual. The sides of the hills covered with luxuriant green, here & there skirted with cottonwood bushes & today increasing to the dignity of trees; also crape myrtle bushes skirting the whole face of the hills.

This morning Dr. White[7] shot Dr. Thompson's[8] horse. He was a vicious horse, an "Original," not lawful to run at large in the States. White had told Thompson twice that he was biting & scaring his horse up & that he could not suffer it & if he was not tied with his head down, or prevented in some way he would certainly shoot him. Going after his horse this morning, White saw the Dr.'s horse plunge at his own & bite him. He then attempted to shoot him but the cap burst & pistol missed fire. Driving them to camp, he shot him just behind the shoulder; he soon died. White went & told Thompson he had shot his horse. Thompson said he would retaliate. White told him "If my horse is a vicious horse doing you any mischief, kill him; if otherwise, & you shoot him, you will have to bear the consequences."

Still ascending the divide, luxuriant green coating the mountains. Just before reaching the top of the divide we entered a strip of woods. The whole train were enlivened, after traveling so long over barren hills without a bush, to enter a strip of rich, beautiful, wooded land—tall spruce, pine, & cotton wood. Emerging from the wood we soon reached the summit. An enchanting scene now lay before us, under as it were though six miles off wound Bear River, looking as a broad silver ribbon spread out in the valley, carpeted with green. Descending the longest, steepest hill since starting, we camped on the Big Muddy, a clear little mountain branch where we camped. It heads a half mile above where the road crossed. Among a variety of flowers beautifying the mountain sides I noticed the queen of flowers the rose, also in abundance the blue flowering wild flax. Tyle & Humphreys[9] came up bringing a fine mess of fish—three speckled trout about 8 inches long & six of a sort we are at a loss to determine the species, from twelve to eighteen inches long. There was a "glorious" mess, more than we all could eat. The boys thought them better than fish at home, attributing [it] to the clear, cold stream. Tyle also killed a duck with which these streams also abound. The Colonel brought in a sage hen, of which there are a great many & on which we luxuriate daily. The alkili has disappeared, there being few streams with any sign of it—to the great joy of all.

Descending the hill to the Muddy there was two roads. Alph Campbell's[10] driver being behind thought he would take the old road as it was nearer & catch the train. Descending until it was impossible to retreat, he came to a precipice some ten feet slant & six perpendicular. They had to take the cattle out & unyoke them before they could make them to descend. Then, rolling the wagon to the slant, Alph stood below guiding the tongue with a log chain, they just let the wagon rip, the tongue plowing the ground & sinking in nearly to the axletree. No other wagon in the train could have stood the jar.

Alvarez,[11] who won some 30 dollars gambling yesterday, remained to gamble with the traders. Johnson[12] remained with him. At noon he had won some 50

Bear River Valley near Soda Springs.

The Diary of Hugh Brown Heiskell

dollars, principally from persons with mule teams with whom we camped. These traders have plenty of money, but of what use it is to them living in these mountains 'tis hard to tell.

We are now in the territory of the Snake (Sushoones) Indians, since crossing Green River. There are none of them on the road. They fear the emigrants, and they are anyhow peacably disposed and would not injure us.

. . . . .

FRIDAY, AUGUST 17, 1849.
LEFT BIG MUDDY.
TRAVELED 16 MILES.

Morning cloudy, threatening rain. The cattle wandered off among the hills, & were hard to find, delayed us until eight o'clock. Traveled 10 miles & nooned on Bear River, a stream some 50 yards wide & 4 feet deep abounding in fish, the speckled trout among others. Mr. Campbell's Aleck[13] brought in a large goose, two ducks, & a Cudlien, a bird of the snipe species, large as a summer duck with a bill about 4 inches long, snipe shaped. There are hundreds of geese & ducks along the river. Our train lives high, having ducks, sage hens, & fish daily. The Colonel killed three hens this morning. Brown & myself rode on before the train to the river. The clouds settling down, there fell a slight rain. Caught a small mess of fish.

The cut off entered into the Fort Bridger road leading up the river valley.[14] This valley is about 1/2 mile broad, level & covered with grass, sage, rushes, &c. Some alkali.

Traveled 6 miles & camped on Smith's Fork, another clear, swift-running stream, abounding in speckled trout—a most beautiful fish, black specks on a dove colored ground. So far as we have seen they are from 6 to 12 inches long. The fork is about 40 feet wide & 3 deep. Although we camped late, Tyle caught some trout.

Alvarez & Johnson came up at dark. Jack played us a trick coming up to the campfire, says he "Did any of you ask me the time by the Lunar time piece"—He had a gold & silver watch, calling the gold the solar & the silver the lunar watch. Pulling out the chain, "Ah," says he, "the hook is shortened & watch has slipped off." "Yes," says Tyle, "it slip[p]ed off at Ham's Fork." "There where I missed it first." "My pistol has slipped out of the belt also." "They got us drunk & slicked us out of every thing except my horse & saddle & a dollar & a half in my pocket." "Well," says the Colonel, "How did Alvarez come out?" "Flat." "He did not lose more than he had previously won, did he?" "Well, about 30 dollars." Alvarez had in fact as we found out won 117 dollars—a slick gambler; Jack, a slicker line.

. . . . .

A fine rain during the night, which laid the dust. Morning cold. Traveled 15 miles; nooned on Thomas' Fork, a stream 35 feet wide, 3 feet deep, not so clear or swift as Smith's Fork. Stopped one hour, having a long drive before us, to reach Bear River again, which bears to the left of the road.

Soon after leaving the creek we began to ascend the mountains It appears that the hills grow worse as we go farther west, for this was the worst since leaving St Jo. After a succession of ascents and descents we are to the summit, looking down on Bear River's silvery water winding among the willow bushes which line its banks. To the left Little Snake Lake lay spread out before us with its outlet running through the valley to the river. Across the plain & river Bear River mountains rise in beauty—Along this range runs Bear River, running north until it gets round the end of them then south along their western base until it empties into Salt Lake. As we looked from the summit on the beautiful plain, after so long & tiresome a drive, I thought of Moses ascending Mount Nebo & viewing from Pisgah height the promised land, & was perhaps as much rejoiced as he, though not as ready to die.

On yesterday Dr. White shot a wolf, the first one killed by our train. Dick[15] killed a badger & Brown a magpie, a beautiful black bird tinged with green with a long tail. It is a little larger than a jay bird. Brown & Nelse[16] also came in with a fine mess of fish—trout; they arrived in camp at ten o'clock. Tyle & the Colonel, who also remained at Smith's Fork, came in at eight o'clock, "luckless wights" with one or two fish.

Before arriving at Thomas' Fork saw Uncle John's[17] train, which drove on before us. Thomas' Creek rises in the mountains to the northeast over 15 or so miles through a fine bottom covered with luxuriant grass, then empties into Bear River, which a few miles before the crossing of Thomas' Fork runs a westerly direction, its general course being north. It here passes through the hills to where we came to it on the plain again ten miles from the creek.

. . . . .

SUNDAY, AUGUST 19, 1849.
IN CAMP ON BEAR RIVER.

Heavy frost. Sun rose cloudless, day warm. What a blessing to have one day in seven to rest, & it always in the right time. Today all are fatigued after yesterday's long march of 25 miles Some of the boys can't resist the temptation to fish & hunt on Sunday. Brown has just come in with a mess of small fish. Dr. White & Nelse have gone down to Pegleg Smiths—two or four miles below camp—to see the Indians & shoot ducks along the river. Tyle determined not to fish or hunt, & nobly has he kept it although the temptation is great when camped near a stream abounding in trout with ducks & geese plenty.

Four o'clock. Camp full of Indians; great excitement. Most of the company trading, blankets for buffalo robes, powder & lead or tobacco for deer skins, lariats, &c. They are up to a thing or two & are not to be cheated as they were many years ago. This year they are well supplied with blankets, ammunition, &c., the emigrants having supplied them. Their trading stock is also low, having sold out nearly. They cross over the Sweetwater in parties to hunt buffalo—which being disputed territory between the Snakes, Sioux, Crows on the north on the head-waters of Green River & the Utahs, south towards Salt Lake. There is a village near us of Bannocks—a portion of the Snakes—so called. They come riding into camp sometimes two on a horse, with a troop of dogs following, which are very troublesome, sticking their noses into everything. The dogs look like a cross of the wolf & fox.

We in some respects resemble the Israelites in their march across the wilderness. Murmuring at the captain when things don't suit us—late starts, short drives, &c. We do not camp in a square with 3 wagons as they did, 3 tribes on the east, 3 on the south, 3 on the North, & 3 on the west, but we move forward in the order which we have finally settled down in, camping in a straight line in the order we drive up. Having fine water & having not murmured at Meribah & having not sent spies to inspect California & therefore having not rebeled at their report, we hope to be so blest as to reach the looked for coast of gold & pearls & not merely see it from the Pisgah height of the Sierra Nevada.

MONDAY, AUGUST 20, 1849.
TRAVELED 15 MILES.
CAMPED ON SMITH'S FORK OF
DOUBLE BRANCH.

Several of us went over to Pegleg Smith's,[18] where the Indian lodges were, to trade. Pegleg lives in a cabin, has plenty of horses, cattle, & money in abundance. We found him a hospitable, honest mountaineer—having been among the Indians ——— years & having a squaw for wife who he calls Mary & who he appears to love. He has peculiar ideas about some things, of course, owing to his habits from so long a residence among savages. On yesterday evening White & Nelse came home & told us that Pegleg had cowhided a fellow for trying to steal one of his horses. It was a large, whiskered man belonging to Uncle John's train. He had remained behind his company all day drunk & quarrelsome. Smith tried to get him off & finally tried to make him go. Having started he was seen driving some of the horses off. They say he was trying to catch one. He says that someone there asked him to help drive them. Oll & Nelse, who were there all the time, believe him guilty. The rest of us think not. At any rate they brought him back and gave him a cowhiding. At dark he came down to our camp instead of going on to his own train. From the talk of White & his reception, he left at daylight. The Indians we found well off, plenty of clothes—coats, vests, blankets, &c., living in lodges made of buffalo skins—not too large or good as the Sioux, although they appeared better off with horses, skins, & money, which they do not know the value of. But they are if anything more uncleanly than the Sioux. We traded for buffalo robes, dressed deer & elk skins, &c. Alvarez bought a horse of good quality for a gun & old coat. I was offered one for my blanket coat, but having enough horses & few coats I did not trade. They gave us service berries, green & dried—also mashed & dried. We saw also divers black and dirty looking messes which they eat but we could not fancy—a root which they boil, dry, & make soup of.

We moved 9 miles from camp, 5 from Pegleg's—a beautiful little creek—Truttuck's—winding among willow bushes through the bottom from the hills on the right to the river. Traveled 5 miles; camped on Double Branch—three branches rising in one place in the hills, separating & running a mile or so apart to the river.

TUESDAY, AUGUST 21, 1849.
LEFT DOUBLE BRANCH.
TRAVELED 16 MILES.

No guard appointed last night & of course the morning guard did not rouse the camp. We all rose late; the sun also, as if imitating our laziness, rose late, making his appearance over the hills after five o'clock. Warm & bright Sultry—no breeze, what we have seldom seen. Decamped at 8; traveled 8 miles; nooned on a small creek, which rises in the hills with another that we crossed 600 yards back. I have heard of the Ganges with its thousand mouths & rivers with their hundred sources but never saw streams from the same source divide & wend their separate course until they discharge themselves in the river. Crossed 3 streams this morning. This bottom & plain is finely watered; streams of clear crystal water, with white limestone pebbly bottoms, crossing it at short intervals.[19]

The fishermen for the day, Brown & Nelse, furnished us with a fine mess of fish.

On yesterday a wagon with four men joined us. They were at Smith's, where they had been several weeks. Crocker's son (the oldest man of the mess, Crocker, not his son, the oldest) being sick & they being acquaintances of Smith's. Tyle & myself do not fancy them, Crocker (son) is still sick & looks as if his stay on earth would be short; his "thread of life is very attenuated."

This evening we left the river, crossed hills eight miles, turned a half mile off the road to the river, where we camped at sundown. Fish for supper. The Colonel & Alvarez, having remained behind fishing, came into camp at nine o'clock with a half dozen fish. On arriving at camp every now & then a flock of geese would rise from different parts of the river & fly over & around us with their peculiar cry, ducks quacking within hearing. The mountains on either hand skirted in places with cedar, those on the left more thickly studded than those on the right. On the former also spots of pure white snow, a small specimen of "perpetual snow." The valley between from 4 to 6 miles. Chilly this evening. Noticed some sprigs of holly; flax scattered here & there, species cultivated in the states.

WEDNESDAY, AUGUST 22, 1849.
TRAVELED 10 MILES TO SODA SPRINGS.

Frost & a little ice. Train started at 6 Oclock. Sun shining hot during the day, but "gentle zephyrs" fanned us"—bah!—making it pleasant & refreshing "tired nature." Remaining at the river, I tried my luck fishing, only caught one trout. Started to catch up with the wagons—which were only going to the Soda Springs which were from information given by Smith only four miles—at half past ten arrived at the springs at one o'clock, finding it ten miles.

These springs are among the greatest curiosities the world affords. Having just returned from visiting them, I would not take half what I expect to make in California for the sights of the day. Crossing the hill country for 18 miles you descend into the valley of the springs. It [is] about 3 or 4 miles across, Bear River running through the middle. Soon after entering the valley you cross a clear stream 20 feet wide one foot deep rising to the northeast & emptying a few hundred yards below into the river. Along this creek are many soda springs, boiling & bubbling as the gas escapes. We camped in a cedar grove about one half mile broad extending from the mountains to the right to the river—where Fremont encamped 25th Aug 43—& a mile below the creek. Here Bear River runs west a few miles past the end of the mountains of its own name, then south. Walking down below camp with Dr. Thompson near the river when some distance from the upper & main spring we heard it bubbling & gurgling, going down we found a basin underground in the rock in which the water was agitated as a violent boiling caldron. then it ran out above boiling & bubbling to the river ten feet off, with a stream 1 foot wide & one inch and a half deep. Just below is another of the same quality, thrown up as the carbonic acid gas escapes. But a half mile below, where a point of the hills comes down to the river covered with cedar at the water's edge, is the Steamboat Spring, the greatest curiosity of all & the greatest in America. It is thrown up a hole in a rock to the height of 7 feet & a half at intervals, sinking below the mouth or outlet & again rising. The jet is a pure white foam [several words illegible] of the rock, which the sulphate of iron contained in the water colors it red & which with the carbonate of lime settles & gradually forms the rock. The rock has probably increased since Fremont was along & Taplin says the "jet de eau" as Fremont calls it is not so high, & that it does not as much resemble the trembling & puffing of a steamboat as then. The name would still be thought appropriate although some of our company did not see much resemblance. While at the Springs the Colonel, Tyle, & Major Bassett[20] came down telling us of a treat they had enjoyed at the Soda Spring—soda water & lemon syrup, the Colonel having provided a bottle for this special occasion. Returning, we finished the bottle. Drinking fine soda water dipped from an exhaustless basin—three thousand four hundred miles travel from home. All pronounced it better than from the best soda fount in America. But with me this seemed to be "all in my eye," for although good & pure, part of the carbonic acid escapes & it does not effervesce so briskly.

．．．．．

Thursday, August 23, 1849.
Left Beer Springs.
Traveled 18 miles.

Morning pleasant. Day sultry. Decamped at 7 oclock. Taking a bucket I rode on with a bundle of clothes to wash. Passing by the springs Dr. White & myself had a fine drink of soda, having a bowl of sugar making it very pleasant; without it, by itself the water has to me an unpleasant taste like soda when it is done effervescing. Filling a bottle with the water we went down to the Steamboat Spring, where we found Major Bassett gallanting Miss Lucy, "Squire" Elliot, & Miss Barnes viewing the strange operations of Nature, putting us in mind of a pleasure party at "the springs."[21] We filled another bottle here to carry back to Tennessee. There were near the spring several mounds, one the size of our Indian mounds rock—the same formation as the one of the Steamboat Springs—a thin shell appearing to be hollow with holes or crevices at the top—it appears to have been formed by a boiling spring gradually until the mound became so high the water would not rise over, then bubbling around the edge of the crater forming the rock until it was closed when the spring would find some other vent. Another mound, 12 feet in diameter at the base 6 feet high with a crater 5 feet across & 3 feet deep, formed in the same way, the spring now extinct. The valley presents the appearance of volcanic action in former times. Comprised in this valley, which terminates where Bear River turns round the mountains 3 miles from where we camped in the cedar grove, is a field of observation sufficient to employ the geologist, mineralogist, and chemist until they would tire with examining nature's works The river instead of running round Bear Mountain it runs through the mountain terminating abruptly on the left, a narrow plain on the right; then the mountains rise again, running on to the head of the valley which opens here to the north twenty miles, where it is terminated by the mountain & spur of Snake Mountains, & 30 miles to the south where the same mountains close on the river forming a canyon, the river turning to the left, valley opening right & left 15 miles across to Grant's Mountain—in the spur of Snake Mountain spoken of. The whole valley shows the effects of volcanic action—ledges of rock with crevices, as if the fire had once burned through them & died out. To the left of the road about a mile is what is called The Crater. It is a mound about 50 feet high 300 yards in diameter, the crater 40 feet deep & 100 yards across, lava rock principally composing the mound, covered with a layer of rich earth. The plain is covered with fine grass except where the volcanic rock appears. On crossing we were much disappointed when arriving at the base of the ridge we did not find a stream of water, having expected to find Grant's Fork here. Entering the hills we did not find water for six miles, where having descended into a broken valley totally surrounded by mountains winding through its willow banks was one of the head branches, the Rose (Roso)—clear, swift, very cold, coming from the mountains to the south where spots of snow deck the sides immediately below the summit & in view of camp. Not knowing the distance the train had neglected to take in water. The Colonel considerately filled some canteens & went back to meet them. After carrying the clothes so far, I commenced washing but having washed six pieces in the icy water I quit until another convenient season. The wagons—with the gee, whoa, haw of the drivers the "go ahead on it there, Patty," a familiar expression of Tyle's—were seen & heard descending the hill to the creek about half past four o'clock. Some Indians encamped above us, one or two of whom paid us a visit.

The sides of the mountains checkered here & there with groups of service berry bushes, loaded with ripe berries. The Colonel & myself fared sumptuously on them at noon, having nothing else to fare on.

The mule teams that overtook us at Green River camped with us this evening. They started from Cincinatti as an organized company, Smith Capt. Quarreled & split up. Another wagon came up at ten o'clock—that had been delayed—there were two men with it. They say that 3 men who were with them, two Dutchmen & a Yankee from Boston by the name of Quensby took 20 days provision & embarked in a skiff that was left by some emigrants at Green river for California.

FRIDAY, AUGUST 24, 1849.
TRAVELED 10 MILES.

Soaked during the night by the rain & again lul[l]ed to sleep by its music as it fell spattering on the tent—disturbed only by thoughts that if it rained long we would be flooded & have to remove to the waggons, which would cool the inspiration of the music of the rain.

Horses strayed & scattered towards the four winds. Train started, leaving some of us hunting for the remaining animals. A steady, heavy rain falling, succeeded in finding all the horses. Drenched with rain, an uncomfortable drive, wading through the mud. The road entered immediately on the hills, our course being direct across the mountains, ridge after ridge rising. Two miles from camp, while descending the hills which we were ascending when we started, the road forked, both being so bad that if we took either we would wish we had taken the other. Finally we cut a road round to the left, & attaching to each wagon 7 or 8 yoke of cattle the train moved forward by sections, two or three going up at a time, then taking the cattle back for the others.[22]

Nooned at the foot of the hills in an uneven valley on another branch of the Roseau, 7 feet wide & 2 deep. We had traveled 5 miles, but by the time the last wagons got over the hills it was one o'clock. Taplin had a glowing fire for us which felt comfortable, being still wet. The rain ceased about ten, sun shining on us at noon. Scenery fine today—the mountain tops hid in the clouds, now displaying more of their variegated surface to view as the clouds rolled up their sides; again hiding them as they thickened down. Across the hills 5 miles this evening—through the rain which had again commenced—to a stream which we called Roseau's Fork, about 50 feet wide & 4 feet deep with a slow current, where we camped. The Colonel, who came on fishing, brought in a large trout eighteen inches long & thicker through than any caught in previous streams.

. . . . .

SATURDAY, AUGUST 25, 1849.
TRAVELED 10 MILES.

Morning clear & cold, wind blowing from the west. Up as soon as it was light, breakfast over & ready for an early start. Soon after the sun in magnificence rose above the mountain among golden coloured clouds of dazzling brightness. Decamped at six o'clock, course south west. Road in excellent order from yesterday's rain, but hilly. We find today that Roseau's Fork—as we called it—that we camped on last night turns to the northwest & must necessarily run into Lewis Fork; it is called Pannack River and empties in below Fort Hall.

The train descended about twelve into a valley of several [miles] width, uneven surface with a sluggish stream of ten feet width running through it. There being a mountain to cross a few miles ahead & no one knowing whether there was water in an evening's drive, and seeing that there was no stream between this place & the mountain we concluded to remain here although there is no wood & we have to cook with sage bushes.

. . . . .

SUNDAY, AUGUST 26, 1849.
IN CAMP.

On waking this morning the sun was shining against the front of the tent. But turning over, thinking "a little more sleep, a little more slumber, a little more folding of the hands to sleep" & was soon again wrapt in "tired nature's sweet restorer." Not long after I was roused by an ineffectual attempt of Tyles to get up, he having roused so far as a sitting posture & again fell back to doze again. When we did finally succeed, the sun had run an hour & a half of its course.

The camp all at rest today, enjoying the luxury of reclining on a buffalo rug— some reading, some writing, and all at times blessing the invention of sleep & practically illustrating that it was not invented in vain. Frank[23] out gunning, killed five ducks; on yesterday, eleven. Wilms[24] killed eight today. Little regard paid to the Sabbath by many of the company. Tyle, although he will curse & swear, will neither fish, hunt, clean his gun, or anything of the sort Sunday. And yesterday, although in favor of traveling until night, when it was proposed to stay until this morning & then go on so as to give us a whole day to cross & find water he would not listen to it

. . . . .

MONDAY, AUGUST 27, 1849.
TRAVELED 18 MILES.

Heavy frost & ice. Last night about ten, there was a regular stampede among the horses, Coming up to camp from below like a tornado, the dogs running out at them, they kept on. The uninitiated thought the Indians had done it & that the horses were lost. But Taplin said let them alone & we'll find them all safe in the morning. This morning two miles above camp they were quietly feeding in excellent grass. Decamped at six o'clock, traveled 10 miles, & nooned on a small branch lined with willow brushes & running south to the Salt Lake. Cattle in fine plight having been in grass since noon Saturday—waist high & thick as the finest oats of a Pennsylvania farmer—in fact, they have improved since entering the basin. Their feet also are well & hardening every day. Saw some wild cherries to-day, the same species as those cultivated in the States, but smaller & not so well flavoured—trees small, 3 inches in diameter the largest. Four miles from where we nooned, we entered in a beautiful valley. Surface uneven, but covered with fine grass, wild flax abundant. Soil very fine—rich & light, slightly gravelly—good for wheat. The mountain sides green with luxuriant grass, quaking aspen, & service berries. Five miles travel west down the valley brought us to a creek running south, lined with willows, skirted with a level bottom two hundred yards wide—black loam, equal to Missouri's best. A few hundred acres such would make an East Tennessee farmer wealthy. Along the branch I noticed some currants, much like those cultivated in gardens—a darker red, rather more acid, but the same flavour.

The Colonel caught some pretty little trout in the branch, although it is not more than four feet wide—average—& one foot deep.

The mule company or a detatched portion of it—Taylor with the steamboat—camped with us.

. . . . .

TUESDAY, AUGUST 28, 1849.
TRAVELED 20 MILES.

Morning cloudy or hazy, the sun occasionally shining through the thin clouds—a real fall day. Traveled eight miles when we entered a valley with a skirt of willows through the middle among which wound a crystal stream over a white, stony bed. Three miles from where we nooned the road entered a ravine, with mountains on each side several hundred feet high on each side. We ascended gradually for about five miles when we reached the summit. The descent was down another ravine but very steep, the sides of the road lined with service berries most abundantly loaded with the finest fruit we have seen, easing the teamsters from duty & driving. But the road was so steep that it required almost incessant watching, the banks on each side to the top of the wagon bed & so narrow that the wheels would rub on either side now & then. Immediately we ascended a small [hill?] where again I came near oversetting; in fact, if Tyle had not held on to the upper side of the wagon it would have went over. My genius certainly does not lie in driving oxen, nor have I as yet been able to find in what it does lie. Having reached the top, Tyle cried out, "The camp in sight; I see the smoke," but on going down to it we were doomed to disappointment, as man's "fondest anticipations are." The infantry had gone on & getting cold had kindled a fire, which spreading out among the grass created considerable smoke. Dick & Nelse who had rode on met us here & told us they had been on some distance & that it was fifteen miles to water, at least. Traveling three miles further, we camped at sundown in a dry valley, rich with fine grass &—to an experienced mountaineer singular—there was no water. The train was poorly provided for a dry country, there being not enough water along to make coffee. Having been caught before without water, all had determined to have some always in their casks, which they kept up for several days & finding water plenty had neglected it again. We had placed our cask to soak last night & this morning put some water in it. On reaching camp we went to it with joy, but it had leaked out, so we were no better off than others, having only two canteens full. Eat a supper of dry crackers & meat broiled on the coals—not having water to clean the frying pan.

. . . . .

WEDNESDAY, AUGUST 29, 1849.
TRAVELED 20 MILES.

Cattle herders drove the cattle into camp by sunup, & having no cooking to do we were all ready. Left in dry mood. The wind rising, soon blew from the north, making it cold even with an overcoat & driving the dust in clouds along the road, which ran south for six miles. It then turned directly at right angles to the west over a ridge, where we expected certainly to find water. On reaching the top Brown cried out, "Twenty miles to water, for I see the road six or eight miles ahead where it enters on a mountain again, & I see some of our horsemen passing along that point, & a mountain looming farther on which we'll have to cross." But soon a horseman came in view bringing glad tidings of joy. Wallace with two canteens of water met us & told us 'twas two miles to water. Having traveled 12 miles, we arrived at a spring to the left of the road. Tyle & Dick were there with two pots of coffee & a good fire—having started on when the train started to have it ready for us—which refreshed us very much after washing off the thick coat of dust which had settled on us.

At two o'clock we resumed our march. The road west still, since turning that course in the morning, and the finest mountain road in the world—occasionally a rough steep hill, but then smooth, with scarcely a rock and generally level or slightly inclined. Six miles from where we nooned, we entered a gorge in the mountains a hundred yards wide—the hills rising on the left a thousand feet, on the right eight hundred—a beautiful hollow with the grass and aspen bushes, the sides of the mountain covered with grass in the "sere & yellow leaf," & luxuriant green of crape mirtle & other bushes. Passing by a spit of aspen, we took in some wood. Two miles from where we entered the gorge, the smoke & light of our camp fire came in view, a small stream of water running down from the left lined with willow & sinking at the wood. Our prudence useless—we had filled our casks, & laid in wood, & hauled them to a camp with water and plenty of dry wood. Eat supper by the silvery light of the moon & the genial warmth of a glowing fire.

. . . . .

THURSDAY, AUGUST 30, 1849.
TRAVELED 16 MILES.

Ice an inch thick in the wash pans, froze in the buckets in ten minutes. Sun rose bright & clear, day calm, noon hot in the sun, pleasant in the shade.

Last night 4 men of the mule co. from Cincinatti, with the "steamboat,"[25] camped two miles above us Came down after our train started to water their mules, so we are now before them.

Myself & the two Whites took a path leading off to the left up a ravine—we supposed it to be a cut off. Soon it commenced ascending an "exceeding high" hill. When we reached the summit a splendid view lay extended before us—a bed of broken hills, cut off by a range of mountains spotted with snow. But the road ran winding far to the right & the path ended here so we had to turn at right angles to our course to get back to the road. An abundance of wild cherries & the finest berries we had seen along the way—these & the view were our compensation for going two miles out of the way.

After leaving camp the road crossed some hills, but those on the right & left still rose several hundred feet above the road. Soon it began to descend a gorge such as we ascended. Three miles from camp, a few hundred yards from the summit, before entering the gorge, on the left of the road were three fine springs, the largest ten feet square, & walled in with logs by the emigrants. Four miles further on we came to another spring which ran down the gorge by the road side, & soon became a bold running branch on which we nooned, having marched eight miles. This evening the branch continued to increase from a tributary or two entering from ravines, and as it increased the gorge widened into a valley gradually, until nine miles from where we nooned, and where the road crosses the branch, a valley six or eight miles wide opens out at right angles to it. This valley is bounded by a mountain running north & south, along which we expect to find a stream & the Fort Hall road. The Colonel & White rode on to see if we could cross the valley in time. Finding we could not, we camped one mile above the crossing or sink where were some willows.

. . . . .

FRIDAY, AUGUST 31, 1849.
TRAVELED 18 MILES.

Morning comparatively pleasant. While breakfasting—sipping our coffee & partaking of an excellent fried rabbit—three men with pack mules rode up, having left Allen's & Turner's 2nd Pioneer Line 75 miles behind.[26] Are pushing on to overtake Jones' train. They gave us some news from the States, having left one month later than we. Reported the death of ex-President Polk and that there were a thousand deaths a week at St. Louis.

Starting across the plain at 7 o'clock, we were much surprised to find it 12 miles to a branch, the willows along the banks of which we could see immediately after starting, and it appeared not more than six miles. Arriving at the branch coming from the south at half past one, we took lunch consisting of a hot cup of coffee, Boston biscuit, bacon & mixed pickles, our usual dinner. The cattle found grass in the branch bottom—a hundred yards in width—the rest of the valley being barren, covered with scrubby sage with scarcely a spear of grass. The mountains bounding the plain still appear several miles off, & to the right there is a gorge down which a stream runs emptying into the one we are on, where we still have some hope of intersecting the Fort Hall road.

Encamped this evening on Raft River, the stream which comes down from the mountain gorge we saw in the morning. It is a clear stream 12 feet broad & ten inches deep, lined with willow bushes. As supposed, we see the Fort Hall road. Our camp is situate in [a] singular green glade—covered with a luxuriant coarse grass—extending some distance from the creek to the left. The artemesia in which we were traveling all day on along this creek this evening suddenly breaks off & the glade commences, and again the sage appears before reaching the mountain.

On the roadside, the three men who came up with us at breakfast (Gay, Smith, & Lowe) had placed a notice for the Pioneer Line, from which it appears that they are going ahead to procure provisions for the Line, as they are scant of that staff of life.

Saw near camp some "Maiden Cane"—so called by Dr. White. It resembles cane, grows about four feet high.

. . . . .

SATURDAY, SEPTEMBER 1, 1849.
TRAVELED 8 MILES.

From the heading of today I see that another month has gone & today is the first day of autumn. The day is very pleasant, a real Tennessee fall day. Morning calm & warm, sun rose bright. Wind commenced about ten from the west, blowing a cloud of dust in the faces of the teamsters.

The valley through which the creek debouches into the plain—which we just crossed & which looked as a narrow gorge—is at its opening one mile wide. As you pass up the stream the road having passed to the right bank you cross several branches coming down from the mountain. I noticed several swampy places slightly covered with a saline encrustation & luxuriant salt grass. One of these— a field of several acres of sunflowers.

The road having crossed again to the left, we halted at twelve o'clock. Taplin went on to see if we would find a camp six or eight miles ahead. Reported that "within ten miles we would not find water, the road leaving the stream we are on." Above camp the creek separates into several forks which debouche from ravines in the mountains, that open around into a plain of several miles width, as lovely as "The vale in whose bosom the wide waters meet."

. . . . .

SUNDAY, SEPTEMBER 2, 1849.
IN CAMP.

Day pleasant. Smoky today, Indian summer appears to have set in, the sun looking singularly red as it does through smoked glass.[27] Brown contends it can't be Indian summer as there is no chesnuts to be burnt for here.

Bean soup for dinner today—which consists of well boiled beans with bacon & is really considered by all as the greatest luxury on the plains, owing perhaps to not having any vegetables

A flare up in camp today. Mr. Thompson was whipping Wash. Thomas running in said "he should not whip him". Thompson said if he interfered he would whip him too, & seizing a hatchet seemed ready to execute this threat. At this stage Mrs. Thomas, rushing in, addressed Thompson, "If you kill my husband you shall not live." Thomas, going back to his wagon, now came out with a pistol. Others now interfered, telling Thomas he had no right to say anything to Thompson for whipping his Negro. "No!" says Mrs. Thomas, "You are in the States, you are not in England." "Well, but what's the difference? Didn't the Americans all come from England!" And so ended the battle.

. . . . .

MONDAY, SEPTEMBER 3, 1849.
TRAVELED 22 MILES.

Decamped at 7 o'clock. The road turned to the left up one of the branches— as it were—of the valley we were in. It was nearly level, slightly ascending. Within 6 miles we came to a small stream which runs into the Salt Lake—meandering through the valley, which seems to be merely a continuation of the Raft River valley & which passes through the mountain that bordered the left side of that valley.

The Pioneer Line came up with us this morning. They are in quite a strait for provisions—the rations being issued, they have just enough to last seven days to their bacon's being out. There are 50 men with 18 wagons, & 40 or fifty extra mules driving along. So if the worst comes they will have plenty of mules to fall back on. Allen says if there is any truth in the report of Polk's death he had not heard it. Sen. Anderson with his company was in St. Louis the 9th of June, horses in bad plight, talked exchanging for mules, vacillating whether to go the overland route to Independence & by the river. They are too late to make farther than Salt Lake this winter.[28]

Nooned on a branch, nine miles from camp. Our road lay west this evening, the valley stretching out to the southwest. Entering the mountains their character became much changed, Whereas they have been heretofore almost destitute of rock—except the Sweetwater Chain—this evening, hills of solid rock appeared, & large isolated boulders of all shapes & sizes. Ten miles from where we nooned the Mormon road intersected the one we are in, at the "Steeple Rock."[29] It is situated to the right of the road & rises in two cones fifty feet high Three miles farther on we found a place to camp. We turned a mile off the road up a valley—which we had just entered—to some willows, that (with scarcely an exception) infallible sign of water. Wood, water & grass plenty. Ten or twelve of us grouped around a cheerful fire of dry willow, waiting for the wagons after dark. The moon just rising above the mountains, throwing a mild light over the valley & opposite mountain, formed a beautiful scene of Prairie mountain life.

I see below us the bright fires of Allen's train—Pioneer Line.

. . . . .

TUESDAY, SEPTEMBER 4, 1849.
TRAVELED 13 MILES.

The morning opened fair & pleasant. The air is most delightful in this country, dry & pure, a cure for all disease. The "aromatic smell" of camphor & turpentine, of the sage with which the air is impregnated also contributes. But there is anyhow

"Purity & freshness in the mountain air
That wealth & bloated ease can never hope to share"

Decamping at 7 we traveled 9 miles over rough hills & nooned on a branch of Goose Creek. Allen's train again in sight, taking lunch below us on the branch.

Camped on Goose Creek, four miles travel this evening. Our tents are pitched on the creek bottoms, a level of several hundred yards width, the road running up it a south course here. In sight of camp and below us is a singular hill, an oblong rounding from 5 or 600 yards around, rising to the height of fifty feet, then level, or rather a slightly inclined plane, covered with cedar bushes. The sides appear

The Diary of Hugh Brown Heiskell

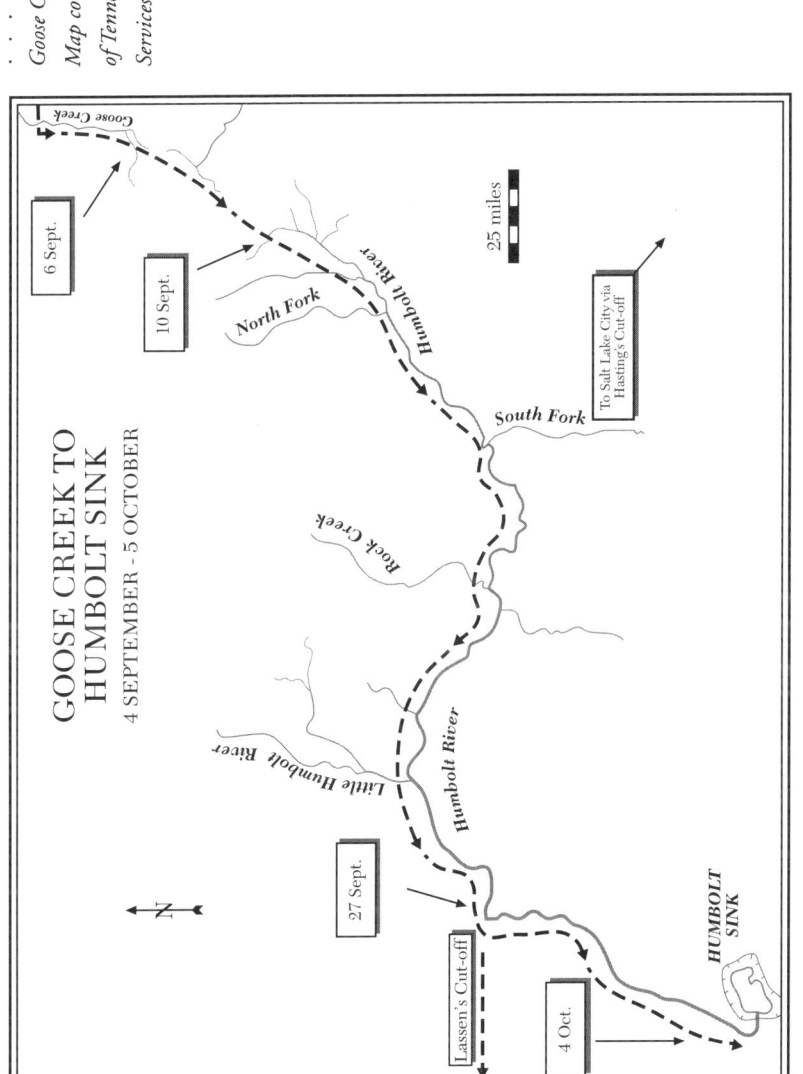

Goose Creek to Humboldt Sink.
Map courtesy of the University
of Tennessee Cartographic
Services Laboratory.

to have been perpendicular rock, but the effects of time & weather wearing away the top it has settled at the bottom, gradually forming a steep ascent, to near the top where the ledge of rocks appears. Upon this step the sage has gained a hold; it scarcely requires any soil, growing in the poorest sand land.

At noon McCourtney's train—with two ladies—were below us on the creek, the same that camped with us Sunday, July 29, on Greasewood Creek, where our oxen were first afflicted with the alkali. They came via Salt Lake, & give a favorable account of the flourishing condition of the Mormons. Their city has one thousand houses, the products of agriculture are abundant, for which the emigrants pay a high price—for instance $16 for one hundred pounds of flour. Green corn, potatoes, & other vegetables plenty, also watermelons. Courtney beat us a little, we entering the cut-off as he passed, but he only lay by 5 days & purchased fresh cattle at Salt Lake. We lay by 6 days & a half.

Warm today. The wind came from the west, blowing the dust in clouds enveloping the wagons & teamsters. Speaking of the purity of the air, it is only pure like the water of the Missouri when it is settled, but when agitated impregnated with sand. Dust in the road 3 inches deep & light & fine as flour.

. . . . .

Wednesday, September 5, 1849.
Traveled 17 miles.

Resumed our march at 7 o'clock up the creek bottom, directly south. On our left along the hillside I noticed large beds of loose stone, a rotten quartz. Large masses, having fallen from the fractured, craggy boulders above, were severed into a thousand pieces as they rolled down.

Having made a good march—ten miles—we stopped to noon although the grass was not very good, what previous emigrants had left being somewhat parched. Alleck brought us up some clams—common mussels—cooked in excellent sauce. They tasted much like the oyster, but were tough, & we concluded they were no great luxury, notwithstanding Dr. Brown's mess (Dutch) eat them with avidity.

We bore to the southwest this evening still on the creek—the road being fine, except the crossing of a muddy slough or branch, & level—then the train came to camp, 7 miles, two hours before sundown. When the train arrives camp presents a busy scene. The cattle turned out, fires are started, water brought. One or two then of each mess get supper, others are pitching tents, others lying on the grass in groups, resting & chatting. The tents being pitched in a row with the wagons some 40 yards off & the fires between, with the different groups scattered around, & the cattle & horses feeding off, forms an interesting scene.

Passed several hot springs. Brown, myself, & White, seeing one near the road, Brown threw down his hat & commenced drinking, but spit it out in a second, not knowing what to think of it. The largest one we saw is about one hundred yards to the right of the road. It is some eight feet in diameter & several feet deep, & with a temperature so high as to be uncomfortable hot to the hand. Farther on on the left along the hill were some singular irregular rock or range of rocks, a soft sandstone worn into various shapes. Cavities worn in the side of the rock, like an urn with one side cut off, showing the inside places resembling the capital of a Corinthian column.

We pass each day several dead cattle. Only one day we have remarked there was none, today. The mortality among mules & horses appears to be increasing for the last week—today 18. Captain Dent's captaincy expired yesterday & the Colonel resumed the duties this morning.

. . . . .

THURSDAY, SEPTEMBER 6, 1849.
TRAVELED 18 MILES.

Morning cool, ice in the buckets. The horses had wandered several miles down the creek, causing the cavalry some delay & trouble. We left Goose Creek which comes from the west, the road leaving to the south up a branch which empties in where we camped. Along the hillsides, through which the branch debouches, I noticed irregular walls of scoriated basalt. Four miles from camp we left the branch, nooned without water on a dry hill. A desert arid country today, one large field of sage, varied here & there on the hills by groups of cedars. Seven miles from nooning, we came to the warm springs valley. On descending the hill which bounds it to the north, we were cheered to see a line of willow winding along the flat. It proved to designate a bold branch of a spring that gushed from a bluff of vertical rock. We were a little deceived on drinking to find it was not very cold— cool enough, though, to be pleasant & healthy. After traveling two thirds of the [way] over sterile barren [illegible word] it was delightful to look upon this clear pure rippling fountain, as its waters played over a pretty bed. Thousands of little minnows appeared to be enjoying themselves in the spring & branch. Running a half mile, it disappears in the sand. As the camp was picked out a mile below & farther down than the branch run, the casks were fil[l]ed with water.

Grass scanty, bunch grass (festuca) on the hills, forming a subsistence for the cattle.

A beautiful & pleasant night, the stars, "an innumerable host", peering from a cloudless sky. A row of camp fires with groups strolling round each in perfectly careless security added cheerfulness to the scene. Gazing at the serene heavens & shining stars, my thoughts turned homeward, & I thought of the placid countenance of a sister, & the stars, as it were her good angels, looking down as a guardian spirit upon her brother in his devious way. Our tents pitched on a dry dusty place, we had dust to spread our beds upon, which although not so sweet & romantic as a bed of roses was perhaps as soft & certainly as dry, and on which we slept as sound as ever queenly lady on "a bed of roses."

. . . . .

FRIDAY, SEPTEMBER 7, 1849.
TRAVELED 18 MILES.

The cattle having scattered in different directions in search of grass, which delayed the train until 9 o'clock. Day quite warm. Some clouds appeared, which were welcomed as harbingers of rain with the joy of the traveler who desires an oasis in the desert.

Traveling down the valley south several miles, the road turned west of south across some rolling country & again entered the valley, which also made a bend, now running south of west. Having made 12 miles, we nooned at some wells, holes 3 to 5 feet deep dug in the dry bed of a stream. Offering the cattle water in the buckets, they were too fastidious to drink. We, not being so nice, drank of water of nearly the same quality. The valley here as you descend into it looks as the bed of some broad dry river covered with dead grass. In the spring it must be carpeted with a rich growth of a coarse kind of grass, which from the dry specimens now grows several feet high, resembling wheat straw. Where we nooned there was a solitary Indian. He had come to the road to trade for powder & lead, &c. Taplin purchased part of an antelope, the remainder of which he had sold to previous emigrants. Making signs, he gave us to understand that he would bring us an antelope for a check shirt. Here we saw the small nut called pinon for the first time. It is somewhat like the goober pea with a single germ instead of two. Passing down the valley six miles—an excellent level road—we camped near some wells with pools in the same dry bed we nooned at for the cattle to drink out of. Here the valley is about a mile wide. The Colonel, being out hunting for grass saw as he supposed as many as one hundred antelopes in a gang, but found the grass scanty. We have lived high for some time past—have antelope for supper, duck this morning, fish last night, & the same the day before.

At an encampment below us are the remains, that is the irons, of several wagons. The non-combustibles are alone left, a "bond[fire]" having been made of all that would burn. The mule harness were good & entire. Men appear on this trip to be actuated by the spirit of the "dog in the manger," destroying what they cannot use, lest it may profit someone else.

. . . . .

SATURDAY, SEPTEMBER 8, 1849.
TRAVELED 12 MILES.

Tyle, having stood the morning watch, had breakfast ready before sunup, & we were ready to start quite early.

Three gentlemen from the States the 26th of June came up with us before starting, & confirmed the report of Polk's death & that Sen. Gaines is dead; also report the death of Cassius Clay. The train started a[t] half past 8, traveling eight miles down the valley parched & dry, the dust rising in clouds as the train moved on, & for miles down the road as far as the eye could reach we could see clouds enveloping the cavalry which were on ahead. We nooned at some small springs running into the dry branch. Grass much better than previous in the valley Looking down the valley from where I am writing, it presents the appearance of a large meadow of some rich farmer, eighty to one hundred cattle feeding & twelve or fifteen horses.

Our whole object this evening being to find good grass to recruit the cattle until Monday, there being excellent grass 4 miles from where we nooned, we stopped several hours before night, having traveled 12 miles today, making one hundred this week. Running by the side of camp there is a branch four feet wide and three feet deep. It runs east to where it meets the dry branch, then south. Here it is warm, supposed to run from a warm spring. The encampment is a pleasant one—dry grass to pitch the tents & spread the beds upon, good meadow thickly carpeted with tall grass, in places encrusted with salt, which being thinly diffused also over the rest of the ground, increases the luxuriance of the grass.

Having washed my clothes, I enjoyed the luxury of a bathe which was no small one, after traveling in the dust, sleeping on, & breathing it. We also unloaded & dusted our wagons out, giving us a Sabbath of unmixed rest.

. . . . .

SUNDAY, SEPTEMBER 9, 1849.
IN CAMP.

As usual the sun found us sleeping. Morning warm, indications of rain, "but all signs fail in dry weather." "The heavens must be as brass" here, for from present appearance of the country it seldom rains. With a delightful breeze blowing, the tent well aired & shading us from the sun, buffalo rugs to lounge upon, so pleasantly situated we would not exchange for the cushioned, mahogany lounge & ventilated palace of the millionaire

A pack train came up & camped just below us. They are from Illinois.[30] There were 130 of them left Independence the 16th of May, with wagons. A man of the name of Kirker, who had been in the Mexican service fighting Indians, was their guide. Near the headwaters of the Arkansas, some of them getting scared employed an Indian guide by the name of John Swanick to lead them across to the Salt Lake road. They dug gold in the Taos Mountains & could average 30 cents per day, concluded it "would not pay" after digging 15 days. Swanick is son of Swanick formerly chief of the Delaware tribe. He brought them through & safe and inspired the company with confidence in him.

Had for dinner today our usual Sunday dish, bean soup, and another luxury, dried apples stewed, a desert that at home we would put down as the last of poor dishes, but here, owing to not eating any fruit, it is eaten with avidity by all & is a luxury.

We are often much amused at mistakes made by Brown. You can not broach any subject whatever, even if he never heard of it, but he will chime in as if well versed in its mysteries. Speaking of Byron, I remarked I knew nothing of Byron except from his poetry & short sketches of his life. "Oh," says Brown, "I have read his life & his travels in the United States," and "Byron is the greatest poet now in the world." Speaking of Pocahontas: "Ah, Pocahontas was a great Indian; there are few such warriors as Pocahontas." From a remark of Bruff's[31]—that from the formation & dip of the strata there was water in a certain location—we in ridicule had made a bye word of it, That from the dip of [word omitted] there was water or there was not. Well, we passed a stream, with banks so level that many <u>thought</u> it ran contrary to the way it did. John swore that the strata dipped 50 feet, from appearance, to the mile in the opposite direction from the way it actually ran, meaning to say in a scientific manner that the plain inclined fifty feet down to the mile, contrary to the way the creek ran.

. . . . .

Monday, September 10, 1849.
Traveled 20 miles.

Morning pleasant, smoky with scattered cumuli. Two miles from camp we came to the head of the creek, a collection of hot springs occupying a space of fifty yards square, forming lagoons, which are covered with a thick scum of sulphur & carbonate of iron. The water is hot enough to scald a chicken. You can not bear the hand in it a second. Around for some distance is a saline encrustation. The place smells like a chemical laboratory, from the sulphurated hydrogen that is constantly escaping. We have doubted accounts of springs near Mary's River[32] so hot that cooking can be done in them, but we are ready to believe any story now about the temperature of springs, if it does not rise above two hundred & twelve degrees.

Traveled 9 miles & nooned at a spring running from some quaking aspen on the right of the road & sinking before reaching it. This is properly the head of the creek as the bed which is now dry to the hot springs is no doubt in wet weather a running [stream].

Major Bassett met with an adventure this morning. Being by himself, some distance from the train unarmed, three Indians with guns came up to him, &, seeing their advantage, took rather more liberties with the Major than he fancied, putting their hands in his pockets, demanding tobacco & powder. Making signs that if they would go with him to the train he would furnish them, he satisfied them until he got into safe quarters.

While nooning, an old fellow rode up from the "west," having left Sutter's the 16th of July. Says flour is worth 8 dollars a barrel at San Francisco & 14 in the diggings; that a man will dig from 25 cents to $1500 a day. The train came in soon of twelve or 13 wagons, with men, women, & children. Going to winter at Salt Lake & then go to the States.

Traveled 11 miles & camped in a beautiful valley through which runs a branch of Mary's River. The wagons arrived at dark. Evening turning very cold. We are [heartened?] to find most excellent grass, for it has a gloomy effect to camp without it, more perhaps through fear & doubt of getting through than feeling for the cattle, though we are not destitute of feeling.

. . . . .

TUESDAY, SEPTEMBER 11, 1849.
TRAVELED 18 MILES.

Morning very cold. Started at 7. The hills closing in, we traveled down a defile through which the branch debouched into a broad valley a few miles below, the mountains rising 5 to 800 feet on each side of the defile. About a mile after entering, the pass became very rocky & rough, large boulders & craggy rock on each side. Here from the base of the mountain on the left burst out a bold spring with a fine, gravelly bottom. The water was very warm, most delightful for foot bathing. In a mile or two the pass opened into a large valley.

Traveled 8 miles & nooned at a spring on the left, near the road, running down to the branch a mile below, seeming to be formed for the accomodation of the emigrants. Tyle & Brown & White had fallen behind fishing in the branch, came up with us here, with 30 small fish. Passing 10 miles down this valley we camped on the creek. The average width of the immediate creek bottom this evening about one mile, & covered with grass—a tall coarse species & a fine small kind, both now in "the sere & yellow leaf." This soil is "kind" & good & affords luxuriant pasturage in the spring, of fine grasses. The cattle are feeding on excellent pasture, grass in seed but not parched. They should luxuriate now, if they knew it, as they will suffer at the sink of Mary's River [Humboldt Sink].

We found a card this evening with the names of H. Hood, A. Hood, A. Hardin, J. C. Hardin, ———— Hardin, B. F. McCarty of East Tennessee on it. They left Knox County several weeks before we did, passed here yesterday. We would like very much to overtake them as they would seem old familiar friends here.

The road, this evening, has been one of the finest we ever traveled on, level as a floor & not traveled enough to make the dust very deep. Yesterday afternoon the road forked; we took the left; the other intersected it a mile above camp. This is a beautiful valley—a line of willow running through the middle, the branch (in this season of the year) in places winding among them, at others sinking in the sand.

For supper a mess of fish—"small fry"—the thirty caught this morning.

. . . . .

WEDNESDAY, SEPTEMBER 12, 1849.
TRAVELED 18 MILES.

Morning pleasant & cloudy. To the left of camp two miles a rather singular and somewhat isolated mountain rises—1500 feet above the level of the plain—from a low chain which runs south along the course of Mary's River.

We had partridge for breakfast. It was twice as large as our quails, & resembles them very much, but of a leadish color owing to their living on the sage; the grouse, rabbits, & all partaking of the color of the sage.

Decamping at half past 7 we continued down the bottom, the road better than the finest McAddamized road in the world. Several miles before us there was a line of willows crossing the plain at an angle of 30 degrees, designating the course of Mary's River. 7 miles from camp we came to the river; dry where the road crossed, lagoons of standing water above & below, the bed of the river about 10 feet wide. A mile or two below a clear bold mountain stream puts in, running from banks of snow in the mountain to the left. Three miles below the crossing we nooned. The river here about 20 feet wide, an average depth of 2 feet. Where the valley of Mary's intersects the branch valley we were on, it is a pretty plain of two miles width. The one we were in, being about 3 miles wide, formed at the intersection a level plain of 5 miles width.

We met a government train with 9 wagons loaded with provisions, & 15 or 20 beef cattle going to Fort Hall, also 15 or twenty horses. There were two men with them from the gold diggings; their account is favorable. We also heard of the Meeks[33] in Oregon. Stephen has gone to California and Joseph Meek is farming. He has an Indian wife who he is now trying to get clear of, as the country is settling with whites, but she clings to him.

Marching eight miles, we camped on the river, here affording less water—an ugly stream, pools along it nearly stagnant, whereas where the stream entered in the morning 'twas remarkably clear & pure.

Cloudy this evening, with thunder & rain & snow in the mountains on our left. Clearing away at sunset we could see the tops covered with a carpet of snow. The sun shone on the mountain side, casting a lurid light along it, strongly contrasting with the gloom caused by clouds on the west of the horizon—this with the pure white snow above was beautiful.

THURSDAY, SEPTEMBER 13, 1849.
TRAVELED 19 MILES.

To the great joy of all it rained last night. Dr. White spoke of how finely he slept, lulled by the pattering rain. So great was its somnorific effect on me that I did not hear it at all. Morning still cloudy, a beautiful rainbow at sunup, with a shower of rain that came near to spoiling our breakfast, which consisted of hot coffee, light biscuit, & fried ducks, & dried apples, stewed for supper last night, grouse, & trout fish. A pack mule train, that came across to Fort Bridger with the train which camped with [us?] Sunday, passed us. They left Fort Smith the 15th of April.

Having made eight miles we nooned. Another slight shower of rain fell on us here. The road is now in excel[l]ent order, there being no dust.

Resumed our journey at half past one. A couple of miles down the valley, a creek came in from the right, through level plain one half mile wide. The creek was clear & about 10 feet wide, one deep. The whole plain is covered with alkali, the grass of a yellow color being impregnated with it, and pools of water standing are the color of lye. A strong odor of lye you smell as you ride across. Emptying into the river just below the crossing, the hills close in and leave a narrow skirt through which the river winds. Here the road heads across hills, leaving the river & again coming to it at intervals. Five miles from the river [the] valley opened out again. The line of willows as you enter it looks as if it covered two thirds of the plain, with its dark green foliage strongly contrasting with the yellow, grass-covered plain & the autumnal-browned mountain. The river makes so many bends back & forth that you see the willow without seeing the intervening spaces, giving it the appearance of being all covered.

We traveled 11 miles, reached camp at dusk. A shower of rain fell on us at dark, showery during the evening. Riding before the train, I saw a cloud passing up the river from which the wagons received a squall of hail.

Game tolerably abundant. Alex brought in a goose & Alph a badger. Several grouse flew up from round camp.

. . . . .

FRIDAY, SEPTEMBER 14, 1849.
TRAVELED 18 MILES.

Morning cloudy. The sun as it rose cast a dim, golden light along the horizon, where the clouds had apparently given place for "his worship" to rise. Wind rose at ten, slight of rain soon after.

Several partridges flew over camp this morning. Tyle shot one on the wing. Dr. Brown shot two cranes on the wing at one shot. We measured one. From "tip to toe" it was 5 feet 11 & between the tips of its wings 6 feet, 10 inches. As the train passed on, Tyle shot a crow, sitting by the road side 50 yards ahead, & as it is in Indian territory he "scalped" him, the bullet completely taking off the top of his head.

Dent & Crocker were riding along the river hunting & came across three Indians (Diggers) in the willows—one of which they brought to the road, a poor miserable specimen of humanity, miserably dirty, with a shirt of fox skins—hair turned inside—which came nearly down to the knees. Naked from there down & barefooted—"true Georgia costume for summer."

Traveled 9 miles to noon. Resumed our journey at one. Evening showery, the sun now shining & now obscured by clouds. The wind has shifted from the south & now blows from the northwest, making blanket coats comfortable. Six miles from where we nooned & 3 from where the road leaves the river & crosses a large hill, a stream discharges itself into the river from a canyon in the mountain on the left, affording more water than the river at the junction. This creek Taplin thinks is Willis Fork. Just before us we have a large hill to exercise the oxen on in the morning. Found two poor oxen here. Splendid supper tonight: grouse, partridge, & fish, which being over Tyle & myself descended from "this poetry of Prairie mountain life" to the reality, & parched some coffee—that dread of little kitchen waiters.

It is a most beautiful night—clear & the stars shining—"all around shone with beauty teeming." Lightning is playing in the east through a cloud that has gathered there, its wavering light contrasting with the steady calm light of the stars.

· · · · ·

SATURDAY, SEPTEMBER 15, 1849.
TRAVELED (18) 17* MILES.

A dense fog this morning; dampening everything a slight shower of rain. It obscured the sun at its rising, but as the day advanced the sun rolled the fog in clouds from the plain & mountainside, displaying the ethereal blue of the azure heaven, & warmth & pleasantness of a May morning.

When the cattle were driven up Dr. Brown's Rum (Rome as he calls him) was missing, which delayed his wagon some time after the train started. The road forked here, one leading down the river valley the other across the hills. We took the latter. Twelve miles brought us to Martin's Fork, where we nooned. Four miles back we came to a skirt of willows lining the banks of a dry branch, the road leading down it south 3 miles to the river. Martin's Fork is also dry. Resuming our march after an hour's rest, we found we were mistaken in relation to Martin's Fork, as we came to that stream two miles farther on—a clear creek, 8 feet wide, one deep. Four miles farther on and one mile from the road, we camped for Sunday, making 18 miles during the day but 17* miles travel towards our journey's end. The yoke of steers we found performed well today. This evening the Colonel found a cow.

. . . . .

SUNDAY, SEPTEMBER 16, 1849.
IN CAMP.

Sun rose fair, at ten o'clock cloudy. Dent & several others, dragging a seine in the river, have caught nothing but a complete wetting. We had fish & chicken (prairie) for breakfast, and corn bread—the first on the trip.

Twelve o'clock. We see Bill carrying little Alex into camp, wounded from an accidental discharge of Bill's gun. They went out hunting. Seeing some ducks, Bill cocked his gun. As the ducks flew, Bill turned around & his gun went off, discharging its contents in Alex's legs about the knees. Dr. Thompson is now bandaging it up without attempting to extricate the slugs—the gun was loaded with slugs.

A fine dinner: bean soup, stewed apples, & would have had rice but Dick set it to one side & it was forgotten. Dick & Tyle were cooks. This morning Humphrey, Tyle, & myself took a bathe in a tepid spring that gushes out of the mountain side & runs leaping over its rocky bed to the plain. The spring rises surrounded with a bed of sunflowers. De Camp, with a mule train, came up this evening. He is the same who was shot by the Sheriff at St. Joe.[34]

. . . . .

MONDAY, SEPTEMBER 17, 1849.
TRAVELED 21/ 20* MILES.

Having found the warm spring so pleasant yesterday, Humphreys & myself, having some clothes to wash took them up there to wash them. The train having to go back a mile to get onto the road, we finished & soon overtook them by making a near cut across the hills. I rode Mag & drove "Ol" the Colonel's horse—his back being sore—& White's horse—he is still lame, having been graveled & drooping.

The oxen Alvarez & Griffith picked up at Smith's was missing. The train started & left Griffith hunting him. Elliott staid with him. Giving up the hunt, they followed the river down through the canyon. They describe it as a wild, rocky scene through, hundreds of ducks along the river. After a rough, wearisome walk they arrived in camp as the train drove up at dusk.

Traveling several miles this morning over an extensive hill we entered a defile leading down to the river. 9 miles from camp & 8* from where we struck the road after leaving camp, we nooned at a small spring that issues from the side of the defile, runs a few steps, & sinks. Resuming our march after an hour's rest, we passed several little springs immediately, into one of which—a miry looking place about 8 feet square—a yoke of Dent's steers stepped in order to drink. In they went, sinking to the tops of their backs. Being unloosed from the wagon, they soon extricated themselves. Nine miles brought us to the river, where we arrived at sundown but found no grass. Crossing the river, three miles lower down we camped where Taplin had found some grass.

The Digger Indians live along this river. They have wicket wigwams made of willows. Sticking down bushes & bending the tops together, they twine smaller willows among these; then they thatch it with grass by merely piling bunches of grass over it, making it in the form of a blunt pointed cone or a bee hive. Those we have seen are about 10 feet in diameter at the base & 6 feet high.

We were amused yesterday at Brown, chatting around the fire. Griffith remarked he did not know that Charles the Second was a catholic, until he read Macauley's history. "Oh," says Brown, "I always knew that certainly he was a catholic I had not called it to mind until you [named ?] it, but I always knew it." This was said in good earnest with as bold a face as if he had read, was well versed in history, when in fact he did not know he was king of England, nor could he tell within 500 years of when he lived.

Tuesday, September 18, 1849.
Traveled 15 miles.

Breakfasted on biscuit made of flour & pinola—half of each—which were very good, & stewed apples, which myself & Tyle, the watch for the two last watches, stewed. While eating, a young man came up from a train camped a mile below, & told us that the Indians on Sunday night had stolen ten head of cattle from them. They followed on Monday their track 15 or 20 miles, but having no horses did not come up with them. The Indians were mounted. He wished us to haul his baggage, which we could not do. As we passed by they had unloaded two waggons which were to be left. The company are principally from Independence. There are two married ladies with them accompanying their husbands—one of them young, polite, talkative, contented, & interesting, the other older, with several _interesting_ little shavers around her.

Taplin, who we left hunting his horse, has come up riding the Colonel's horse. He supposes his horse is stolen, most probably by some emigrant. I saw from the road an excellent government wagon, complete in all its parts, left perhaps by the rifle regiment for Oregon. Having made 8 miles we nooned. Our friend who wished us to haul for him this morning is with us packing, he has about 40 pounds carrying on his back. He started with McNulty's train, which threw away their wagons there in order to pack. Himself & a partner had several mules which gave out, & they were left, falling in with this Independence train. They have been traveling with it. Quarrelling this morning, this young fellow has come on, leaving the two broken down mules to his partner, packing a bundle of some forty pounds

Having traveled 7 miles we camped at 6 o'clock. We drove our cattle out from the river for the double purpose of guarding them against Indians & there being good grass. We commenced this precaution tonight—3 persons on guard at a time, & three watches. Passed another good wagon by the roadside.

Our packing friend, whose name is Ludlow, was relieved of his burden by Mr. Howard. He gave Mr. Howard a good Colt's revolver to deliver his bundle in California, who is to give Johnson 15 dollars to haul it.

We saw several magpies flying among the willows. It is a beautiful bird, its body being black, with a long black tail; its breast white & the half of its wings next the body, and the tip of the wings black.

WEDNESDAY, SEPTEMBER 19, 1849.
TRAVELED 16 MILES.

Last night the cattle guard for the first watch—three Dutchmen[35]—in driving them together they started towards camp & the river, where they arrived before the guard headed them, stalking among tents & wagons with their bell ringing & the guard hallooing.

Campbell's wagon did not come up last night, having delayed, in order to exchange his wagon for one left by the train that lost 10 oxen. He is not with us today noon. Ludlow tells us that the Dutch train—which we saw on the Platte & with which Dr. White & Nelse had the adventure about a mule—came by the Salt Lake & entered Hasting's cut-off, where they would have to go 70 miles without water. Not believing that there was no water, they made no preparation for it. Going 40 miles they turned their cattle out to hunt water in the desert. Three men had got through & were returning with water.

The valley is improving as we descend the river. The whole of it is rich, but heretofore generally parched up. It is of a light, ashy soil, horses sinking up to their fetlocks at every step unless where a sod of grass bears them up. This evening the valley has widened out to some 8 miles extent & is not so arid. Along the river it wears a luxuriant appearance, grass greener & fresher than previously.

We have a most excellent camp tonight—all satisfied, which is rare—wood plenty, water convenient, & a fine meadow in sight & hearing of the wagons.

Tyle & Humphreys, who went across the river hunting, came in with five partridges, one duck, and a badger. The Colonel has also killed a couple of the former.

Mr. Campbell's wagon has come up with us. The road level today, but dust six inches deep. We are like the Israelites; if not led during the day by a pillar of cloud, we travel in a thick cloud—of dust—and if we do not have a pillar of fire by night, we have bright willow fires burning in camp.

THURSDAY, SEPTEMBER 20, 1849.
TRAVELED 17 MILES.

Morning cool; day hot & sultry, a fair specimen of several previous days. The wolves were howling all round camp during the morning watch. As the cattle were being driven up two horses were missing, Doc & Johnson's. The train moved on, leaving the horsemen & some of the footmen hunting for them. We searched up & down the river among the willows—which are so thick that you can not see ten steps through them. One by one the hunters followed the train & gave up the hunt. Doc went to the wagons, got some provisions, & went back. All tried to prevail on him not to go as there really was danger, for he intended to follow the tracks and if it was Indians he would stand very little chance. Neither would he listen to Dick or anyone else accompanying him.

There was little grass for the cattle at noon. Doc's place was vacant at dinner. We are uneasy about him. Dick talks of going back, but as it would be doubtful about finding him he did not go. This evening along the road he found a track which without doubt must be Ol horse's track, as he was shod behind & not before, and Dick was on before any person had passed today, so it must be some scamp going to California who has stole him. The road fine today, & this evening there was little dust, the road being firm & hard. On both sides the plain is white with alkali. Our camp is again favorable for grass, water, wood, & guarding the cattle. While sitting around the fire eating supper, we were agreeably surprised to see Doc come in. He had found the same track Dick followed this evening & saw that he was on before. Since dark, as he was coming on, he heard the willows breaking. Stooping down, he saw two figures issued from them and advanced across the road, where he thought they stooped down. Mustering courage—for he says that he never was so scared in his life—he fixed his gun, got out some extra bullets for quick loading, & advanced, but whatever it was had disappeared. During the middle watch the horses were seen; they were therefore stolen this morning during the last watch, Bassett, Brown, & Wallace Barnes on guard. They walked around the cattle once & then sat by the fire until day, and are quite ashamed of the way they kept guard.

. . . . .

FRIDAY, SEPTEMBER 21, 1849.
TRAVELED 17 MILES.

Waking this morning I heard ducks quacking in the river nearby, greeting my ears as a familiar morning scene at home. But I had been too long from civilization, & too far out among the mountains to be carried back very vividly. Soon sportsmen were among them shooting, and ducks were flying over camp in all directions.[36]

Another watch was added last night, commencing at dark, then until ten o'clock. So far the cattle guard have proved rather a humbug, most of them, preferring to sit by the fire to walking round the cattle, exercise this preference during part of their watch, leaving them to guard themselves.

The road left the river a few miles this morning, where the river runs around a hill—to the south—which appears to rise in the plain, which extends level several miles north. Passing this hill we saw the river wending its way a few miles before us, & were glad to see the Colonel & Taplin and their horses unsaddled where we were to noon, as it was now one o'clock. The plain is for a mile or two skirting the river on each side covered with grass; outside of this, to the mountain bare several miles, is covered with greasewood & alkalic encrustation, the mountain covered with short, shrubby sage. At divers places we have noticed this. Greasewood in the medium, between the grass & the sage. Although sage would be called the characteristic, the former occupied a conspicuous part. Our picked-up yoke of cattle have given out. "Thunderbolt," coming into camp last evening with "colors trailing," was left quietly pasturing by the riverside, lord of hundreds of acres of grass, until bowled over by some Indian or wolves. Humbolt lay down in the yoke this evening & would not get up, & was left lying to use his own pleasure when he should rise. Our friend young Crocker, who was unwell when he joined us at Smith's, is recovering, being able to ride his fine little pony although still weak.

. . . . .

SATURDAY, SEPTEMBER 22, 1849.
TRAVELED 15 MILES.

Tyle, myself, Johnson, and myself were in the last or morning watch. Hearing a mule braying as we started out and finding our own mule near camp, knowing there was no other in company, we were a little puzzled. Going down to the river we heard the quick, hurried step of some animal crossing. Advancing with caution and stopping now & then to listen, Tyle whispering "dont speak," we heard, as it got out among the willows, the steer eating, which relieved us somewhat & amused us considerably. It was a beautiful morning, clear & cold. The stars, the "poetry of heaven," spread out in all their wild beauty. And Venus—the Queen of stars, and brightest jewel decking the heavens—shining in the east, the forerunner of day, then Mercury appears just below Venus immediately preceeding the light of [morn?]. Then a streak of light along the eastern horizon soon eclipsing the light of the stars, first the Milky way and smaller stars disappear, and lastly Venus modestly retires as if ashamed to shine in the face of the sun.

Eight miles from camp we entered the hills; the river passing through the hills to the left. Five miles brought us to the river again. It was now three o'clock, the day being hot and sultra [sic] as the climate of Alabama at this season of the year. We had made slow progress. One of Captain Dent's steers fell down dead, & one of Campbell's died.

We saw a notice from DeCamp, which said they had been attacked & were in great danger, but escaped without hurt or loss. The paper was torn, & from the fragments we could not tell by whom he was attacked, whether by Indians or white men—most probably the latter.[37]

. . . . .

SUNDAY, SEPTEMBER 23, 1849.
IN CAMP.

We were astounded this morning, while yet in bed, to hear persons outside of the tent say that old man Crocker was dying. In a few minutes he was dead. He had been sick a week or ten days, but no one thought seriously. His son, a boy of ———— years, is left alone in the wide world, hundreds of miles from "home & friends & kindred dear." He is very weak, having not yet recovered from his long sickness. If he should regain his health it will go hard with so delicate & youthful a boy to buffet the storms and ills of life and elbow his way, until he can make his way to his home again.

We spent the morning digging the grave for Mr. Crocker. Having seen divers bodies exhumed by the wolves, we dug it deep. The corpse lying in camp all day, although none seemed to be affected by the death there was no hunting going and not much noise in camp. The place selected for the grave is a pretty spot, with a fine bush (of the hawthorn species) shading his head, and some on each side and others at his feet. As the sun buried itself behind the mountains, we buried him whose sun has set forever on earth; when it rises tomorrow it will shine upon his grave, far from the habitations of civilization, his peaceful slumbers only troubled by the stealthy tread of the Indian or the howl of the wolf.

A pack mule train passed us this evening. We also see a train of wagons in a cloud of dust passing on. The train from whom the cattle were stolen have come

up & camped above us, and a small company, 8 persons with 7 riding horses and one wagon with four horses attached. They told us of two persons two or three days back now with a wagon, who we suppose to be Cash & Anderson Alex Campbell is improving fast. We hope he will recover without serious, or lasting injury from his wound, and prove a warning to him, that will break up his hunting on Sunday, and make him more careful.

MONDAY, SEPTEMBER 24, 1849.
TRAVELED 17 MILES.

As the train started Tyle rode up to the camp of the train above us, to purchase some flour, as they had more than they could haul since losing their cattle. He bargained for two hundredweight, at eight dollars per hundred.

A large mule train of some 65 men and perhaps an hundred mules have been with & passing us during the day; part of them are camped above us tonight. They are from all parts of the Union, & started from Fort Smith the fourth of April, with ox teams, and from Santa Fe they packed across to the Salt Lake by the old Spanish trail. They had an adventure with the Utah's [*sic*], about one hundred miles before crossing Grand River. About 50 came up to them & made signs they wanted to trade. The train moved on with them, [humoring?] them until they came to a stream where the Indians had camped. Not having anything to trade the train moved on. Soon, while passing through some cedar bushes, a rifle was fired, and a second, wounding one of their mules. The Captain now ordered them to an open place, the Indians galloped round but did not come within gunshot. Hoisting a white flag, the Indians came in. Peace was made. The chief gave them a horse in place of the mule they had wounded. Blankets were swapped for horses, and other trading done. The train now moved on unmolested. We get from them a correct account of the Dutch. Starting through Hastings' cutoff—a distance of 70 miles without water, and almost destitute of vegetation, the sage not growing there, a salt encrustation covering the ground—having got their wagons 40 miles, their ["cattle" omitted ?] gave out and were turned out to die. The blood of the dying cattle, and of others that were killed for that purpose, afforded some relief to the suffering men. They all got through, & saved six or eight head of cattle, also a cart with them. They now intend to pack all the provisions in the cart that it will haul and each man pack some on his back.

'Tis warm and cloudy tonight, but we fear that the "heavens are as brass" above us, for in this country it is like it is "in dry weather all signs fail."

. . . . .

TUESDAY, SEPTEMBER 25, 1849.
TRAVELED 16 MILES.

The mornings are now cool but pleasant, days very hot Last night the cattle being across the creek, Squire would not cross over when on watch, and is hereafter to be passed over, so that it may not be said that he stood watch when he sat by the fire all the time.

The train that we engaged for the flour with not coming up, last night White, Tyle, & Humphreys stopped to get it & pack it up on the mule. About ten o'clock today we struck a deep sand which retarded the wagons & fatigued the cattle so that we had to water them, which we seldom do between resting places.

The mountains are closing in & contracting the valley, until this evening it properly consists of the immediate river bottom only, the hills are then a bed of pure sand. To avoid the heavy pulling through this sand we crossed the river late in the evening, and kept along the bottom where it is of the same light dusty nature as heretofore. Passing down the south side, sage hens or grouse were abundant, wild & hard to get [a] shot at.

By sundown we had made 16 miles and camped. Grass was not very good or plenty; wood scarce & small. At nine o'clock we heard Tyle hallooing over the river. We answered him & soon they found the way to camp, Having waited until this morning and the wagons not coming up with the flour, Doctor went back and found them, where we nooned yesterday, cutting grass for the northern route, and razeeing a wagon.[38] Putting two hundred pounds of flour on the mule, White walked and drove, it being eight miles back. When he got to where he left the boys, 'twas late. They now started afoot and had a long walk to camp.

We begin to tire of Mary's River, although it is a pretty enough stream, clear and tolerably cool, the thick willows keeping the sun out to some extent. But then it is the same monotonous scene—a dusty road, a line of willows, and hills covered with sage. The valley looks as if "walled on all sides round" with hills, before & behind & on either side.

. . . . .

WEDNESDAY, SEPTEMBER 26, 1849.
TRAVELED 17 MILES.

Decamped at 7 o'clock, Recrossed the river and nooned a mile below, having traveled 8 miles, Two men—packing, but with a four-horse wagon, that came up to us last Sunday night—took dinner with us.

We crossed the river again this evening, the main, old road leading down the north side. As several of us walked down before the wagons, we could see what looked like a road leading up a ravine across the mountain to the north, we thought perhaps the South Oregon road. For some time it has been under consideration whether or not to go that road; it being a lower pass there would be no danger from snow, but then it is 70 miles farther.[39] Not being able to get any reliable information respecting it, it was concluded to go the old route by Truckys Pass, with which Taplin is well acquainted.

Crossing again, we camped on the north side. Here we found some large hawthorn (vulgarly called bullberry bushes) growing on the opposite side of the stream

. . . .
The Humboldt River near the beginning of the Lassen Trail.

and some killed by fire. These made excellent cooking wood and the largest bush wood we have seen on the river.

Frank was in a pet at dinner. He is a good, honest, clever Dutchman. Mrs. Thomas had scolded him about whipping the oxen. In fact she is always talking and will not let Frank drive without troubling him. This evening old man Thomas took it up and passed some boisterous words between him and Frank to the amusement of camp. Frank in high du[d]geon would not eat his supper. Mr. Thomas came up to our fire to talk it over. "Ah," says he "It distresses Anna to death. Her feelings are so tender that it makes her cry, 'til she must break her heart. With me it would not matter, but Anna is of so delicate a feeling she can't stand it—for I think a man a fool to fall out with his [girl?]."

As the train came up, the dust was very thick and hung over the camp in a cloud, there being no breath of air to move it off, which until coming on this river we were strangers to, for there was a wind blowing every day.

· · · · ·

THURSDAY, SEPTEMBER 27, 1849.
TRAVELED 17 MILES.

Made an early start this morning, At noon, having determined to leave the cart, we set to work making the necessary arrangements. By so doing we have a team of four yokes and an extra yoke resting, thus the team may be recruited for the 40 mile stretch and the mountains. We put everything that was much needed in the wagon, and took the cart wheels off and put them on in place of the on[es?] on the wagon, they being stronger. The destruction of property has been great down the river—irons of burnt or destroyed wagons scattered everywhere. A wagon would be poor sale here; in fact, I have seen a good wheel broke up to cook a cup of coffee. Saw a stove which must be the "last," for from the number seen they must have run out. Campbell's team has given out, and can pull their load no farther. They worked at noon to fix the cart to bring it on until night, intending to take it in place of the wagon. Mr. Thomas took the wheels we left in place of his in which the spokes wobble, or are loose. These were put on the cart, and Bassett with a yoke of oxen started to bring it on. One of the oxen was [one?] picked up and then gave out, and he had to leave his cart 3 miles back. What's to be done, I know not. They can go no further, and we cannot wait until the cart is brought on tomorrow and the change made.

Just below where we are camped the South Oregon road leads off. Taplin and the Colonel were down there at five o'clock this evening, and saw McCourtney there, and his train moving on. He came in before us at Steeple Rock with fresh cattle from the Salt Lake and had traveled every Sunday. His cattle are broke down. He says they cannot pull up a hill of any steepness, & for that reason he takes the road round to avoid the mountain. At the forks of the road are a great many notices.[40]

Grass very scarce tonight, which makes us uneasy about pasture below.

. . . . .

FRIDAY, SEPTEMBER 28, 1849.
TRAVELED 14 MILES.

Decamped at eight o'clock. Traveled 8 miles and nooned. The crackers have given out. We fried some "slapjacks," a very common edible on the plain, which with some cold biscuit formed our dinner.

On yesterday, as several of us walked along the bank of the river—off the road—we came to a rattlesnake den or town. Tyle was before and called our attention to a very large one, asking Elliotts for his pistol—an article worth a dollar and a half and shooting with as much accuracy as a cork for a barrel. I tried to shoot it, but the snake, "smelling a mouse," commenced disappearing in a hole. The pistol snapping, it escaped unhurt. There was divers tracks where many snakes had trailed in the sand. In a moment Tyle called out, "Here is another," larger than the first and the largest we had seen on the trip, being about 3 1/2 feet long. Shooting at it, Tyle crippled it, and there was neither rock or stick near or anything whatever to kill it with, & not another load for the pistol, so the ["snake" omitted?] rolled down the bank some 20 feet into the river and swam across. Along this bank the land had fallen down in masses and given way, leaving crevices in which they sheltered.

Passed the fork of the South Oregon road and the old Trucky Pass road. Took the latter, leaving our names among perhaps an hundred other notices left by previous companies.

Muskrats are abundant along this stream; saw several this evening, and a weasel.

We left our noon halt about three o'clock, where grass was again scarce, Taplin moving on ahead in search of better camping for the night. Being before the train we saw the Colonel coming back in a lope. He had also started after Taplin, to tell us to take in water as there was grass ahead but off from water. Here we left

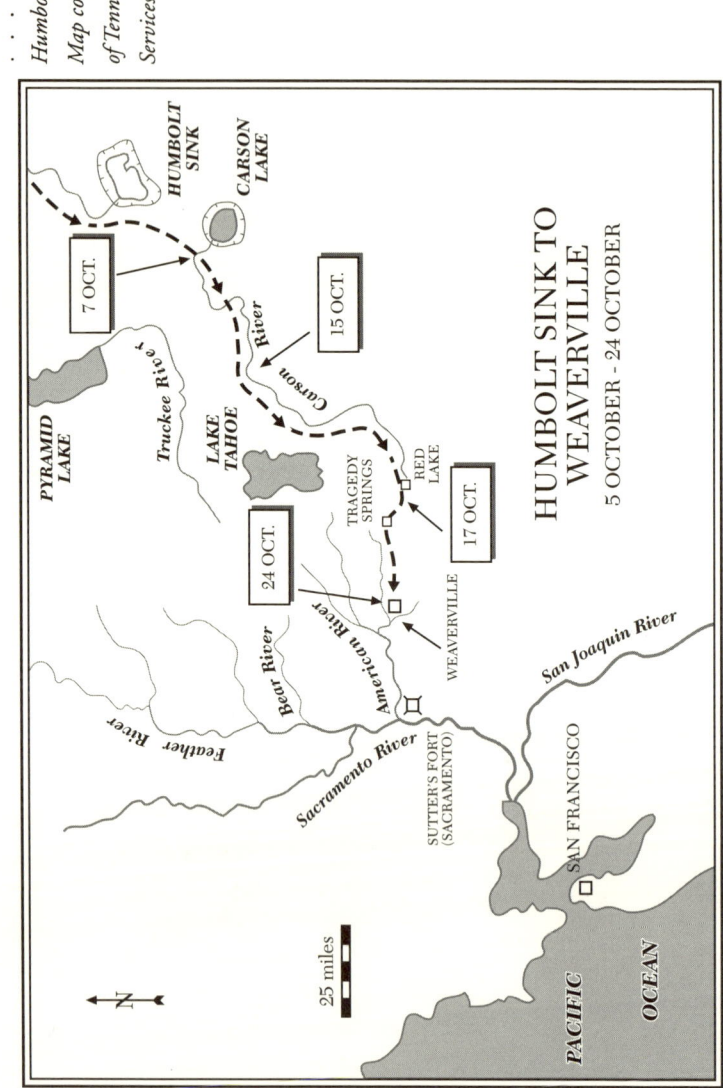

Humboldt Sink to Weaverville. Map courtesy of the University of Tennessee Cartographic Services Laboratory.

the river, traveled six miles, and camped in a level, dusty sage field, where there was some little bunch grass.

The clouds, which had been threatening rain for a day or two, gathered thick at dark with slight thunder and lightning and a hard south wind, indicating immediate rain. Our tents were blown down, the pins having a slight hold in the porous earth. The dust was sweeping, filling your eyes and dusting the supper. The wind blew and the dust sprinkled, but the rain did not fall. Night was fast passing off. We were all sleepy, afraid to sleep out for fear of rain, and could not sleep in the wagon as it was [illegible word]. But, finally, it being so uncomfortable in the dust and wind, we got into the waggon. Nelse piled down with his head on a trunk, his body on some sacks, and his feet like the fellows with ["tieing shoes loose"?]. Tyle crowded up with his feet over the side boards, myself sitting up with my head in a bundle of bed clothes. Our positions not inviting sleep immediately, we talked, laughed, and sung until about 11 o'clock. The wind ceasing, we pitched the tent again, spread our beds, and enjoyed the luxury of sound sleep, "tired nature's sweet restorer."

The Colonel found an ox where we left the river, which was brought to camp and turned with the other cattle. But this morning he was gone, and with a half hour's hunt could not be found. He had perhaps struck back to the river for better pasturage.

We no longer see any traces of Indians. The country is too poor for even the miserable Digger Indians to live. The valley has opened out to an expansive level, covered with sage and not a spear of grass. The immediate bottom, narrow, and ten or twenty feet lower than the common level, is now parched, but in the spring is covered in places with grass. There is a ridge or range of mountains bounding the plain and parallel with the river, which produce the shrubby sage alone. We have noticed there is not a spring or stream emptying into the river since Martin's Fork. Our water has here an alkaline taste, which increases daily. The road today bore to the south, and for several days our course has been south of west.

. . . . .

SATURDAY, SEPTEMBER 29, 1849.

TRAVELED 12 MILES.

Taking a hasty breakfast of "slapjacks" this morning, we decamped, and moved on in search of grass. We took a right hand road which led us to the river in about three miles where was a little of this "staff of life." Here we staid until half past ten, then traveled on to find a good Sunday camp, a drive of nine miles over the same desert, dry country brought us to the river again. Here was a miserable place to camp, dust 3 inches deep, a vigorous growth of greasewood, but very little grass, which will force us to travel tomorrow. For wood we have the bed & woodwork of a wagon, left by previous emigrants.

We turned the cattle to the hills where was some bunch grass, but so scattering that the cattle wandered about, and in the night they came down into camp before the watch.

. . . . .

SUNDAY, SEPTEMBER 30, 1849.
TRAVELED 15 MILES.

Camp in a bustle this morning—cooking, striking tents, and preparing for a start, but made a late start owing to the cattle being much scattered. Traveling 8 miles, we turned off to the river and nooned in sight of it, but could not drive the wagons to it, the level we are traveling on this morning being much higher than the bottom and a steep descent to it. The cattle were driven down to water and graze on scant grass. We dined "sumptuously" on cold biscuit, slapjacks, & coffee. The Colonel was not with us at noon having gone on to look for grass.

Driving about seven miles and a half, we followed a left hand road to a secluded valley in the bend of the river, which the Colonel had selected and where grass is plenty. The train coming in after dark, lighted by a bright shining moon, found wood gathered for each waggon by the usual "forerunners." One of the oxen belonging [to] the Dutch gave out and they did not quite make the camp.

. . . . .

MONDAY, OCTOBER 1, 1849.
IN CAMP.

Situated in a horseshoe bend of the river, our camp is very pleasant. It is an open place, covered with a carpet of grass and surrounded with willows.

The Germans came in this morning, and it was concluded by the company to stay here today and recruit the cattle and give the Dutch an opportunity to make a cart. Camp presented quite a busy scene, today all lightening their wagons. Campbells making a cart, Thompson razeeing their wagon. Thomson [Thomas?]

working on his and Barnes piddling at his. Some Indians came in and were put to smoking skins for us. They were well dressed in clothes given them by emigrants, and are willing to work at any thing you wish them. Make signs to them to bring wood and they will dash off and soon return with a load; point to a bucket and the river, and they will bring you water.

We had for dinner today a Dutch dish of Tyle's make. It consisted of apples stewed with bacon and dough rolled thin cut in small pieces and put in it. Upon the whole it was very good, and we did it full justice.

The Germans finished their cart, threw away their [omitted word], and many other articles. They had had an excellent outfit but had not paid enough attention to the weight of their load. Campbell has finished his cart, a clumsy, heavy vehicle little better than his wagon.

The Indians late in the evening gathered together different little articles given them and left us, all but one old man, who lodged with us, sleeping outside of the tent with a blanket to cover with. This has been a harvest time for the Digger Indians—they call themselves Piyutes. So many teams have failed that an immense number of articles of clothing, &c., have been thrown away here.

. . . . .

TUESDAY, OCTOBER 2, 1849.
TRAVELED 12 MILES.

Tyle and myself rose before the stars disappeared. It was the coldest morning we had witnessed. The Indian getting cold, had struck off and brought a load of wood to make a fire. He would not burn some that we had lying convenient. We were all ready for an early start and turned out among the willows to help with the cattle. Getting them yoked up, we got off at half past 7 o'clock. One of Mr. Campbell's steers was missing. After hunting until they despaired of finding him, Bassett gave the Indian who staid with us a blanket, and he soon had the ox "forthcoming."

Traveling midway between the river and the hills, on each side of us was a broad field of greasewood. About eight miles from camp we crossed a sluice of the river, which had rushes and other vegetable matter decaying in, from which continuous bubbles of carburetted hydrogen arose, sending forth its peculiar smell. Four miles further we came to the place selected to stop, where we arrived about four o'clock and found the Colonel stirring hay.[41] We have to take in [feed ?] for the teams across the forty mile stretch. Some previous emigrants had left a pile of hay, and there were several Indians here who the Colonel & Taplin employed to cut and carry across a sluice of the river on which we camped, grass. Just give one of them a knife and point over towards the grass and he would start over and soon return with a heavy load of long grass, about 3 or four feet long. The river bottom here is rich, an expansive meadow of luxuriant grass with divers sluices of the river running through it. The second bottom is nearly on a level with the immediate bottom, and covered with a crust of salt, and very large greasewood bushes, among which is growing in many places a dark green, vigorous [kind?] of salt grass.

· · · · ·

WEDNESDAY, OCTOBER 3, 1849.
IN CAMP.

Morning very cold, and we were not oppressed with heat at midday, the sun's rays only making it pleasantly warm.

We went to work, in order to start at one o'clock Cooked provisions for the dry stretch, so as not to use water for cooking and other necessary arrangements. But the Dutch and Campbell wished to recruit their cattle today and we have waited on them although a day to us now is invaluable, and may cost us serious trouble and danger. Our camp was filled all day with Indians, ready to do any thing you wished them, provided you gave them some "hogament" (as they call it) or beads which they prize higher than any thing else and much higher than

· · · · · · · · · · · ·
Big Meadows at Lovelock, Nevada.

any Indians we have seen previously. But they have nothing to trade, no horses at all, no moccasins to sell; some of them have them to wear. They are miserably poor, but now well clothed.

Our camp today has looked like a hay meadow, grass scattered all around, someone stirring it, others carrying more, and the Indians employed in this way.

The horses were hard to find. Colonel, having a summer coat, gave it to the Indian who staid with us night before last, and he went out and found all but Colonel's Oliver, Louis' horse, Crocker's pony, and Greg's horse. These were not found until too dark to look for them.

At sundown a pack mule train came up and camped below us. They are direct from the diggings, having left the settlements 10 days ago. Their report of the abundance of the gold is favorable enough, but they say provisions are enormously high—flour, coffee, and sugar, each 3 bits a pound. And say that with industry and economy you can clear from 3 to 6000 dollars a year.

There is with us tonight an Indian who says he will go with us to California.

. . . . .

THURSDAY, OCTOBER 4, 1849.
TRAVELED 14 MILES.

A real wintry morning this, cold and a north wind blowing. The missing horses were not forthcoming this morning, and about the time the train started, their trail was found going back in the road. Tyle and Colonel B. mounted on the mule and Mag have followed in pursuit of them.

Our Indian is with us this morning, making fire, bringing water, &c., but when the train started he went back, making signs that he wanted to go and get a wife he had left & so vamoosed, taking with him a saddle blanket we had given him to sleep on. We traveled six miles down the river plain, and took lunch at "the wells," a grassy flat where are about 12 holes dug, in which is cool water. Our lunch consisted of cold boiled beans and bacon, and cold biscuit. There were about the same number of wells as at Elim, "And they (the Israelites) came to Elim where were twelve wells of water, and three score and ten palm trees, and they encamped there by the waters." But at our Elim were no palm trees and so we did not encamp. A sight of trees would feast our eyes, as we feast them in the spring on the cheerful green, after the monotony of winter's nakedness.

We traveled this evening for several miles through a wide field of maiden cane

(Arundo). It was dry and in places burnt off recently. The fire burns down into the roots several inches below the ground, which is porous. The road then entered a space of some two miles diameter, as level as the bosom of a placid lake, which looks like it has been covered with water. In fact from the immense number of small shells—snail shells of various sizes and shapes—a great part of this valley appears to have been flooded. And from the general appearances and formation of the valley it is a reasonable supposition that formerly was here a great lake like the Salt Lake, and that some internal commotion has opened a way of escape for the waters, leaving the river—the lake's original source—to wear its channel and sink in the same way.

Part of the Dutch train that was with us on the Platte and who lost their cattle on Hastings' cutoff are camped with us.

. . . . .

FRIDAY, OCTOBER 5, 1849.

I rose this morning before it was light, to secure clear water for the cattle before camp was roused to muddy it, and drew and filled all the vessels, but the cattle would not drink it. Waking Humphreys, we cooked slapjacks and had breakfast ready early. The train started as the sun rose above the hills, Griffith and Cockerill looming out ahead.

The Dutch who encamped near us last night are in a piteous condition. There are 7 of them, with two miserable horses, so poor they can scarce walk. On these is packed their plunder. They have also a poor cow which they picked up & which will fall by their "tender mercies" in a few days, as it is intended for beef. A few days ago they were constrained to kill a horse and use [it] to live upon. Some of our train have furnished them with divers articles of provision. Barnes gave them some rice, pinola, coffee, &c., and as long as they stay near us they will not suffer.

Seven miles below camp the road forked in a flat a few feet above the level of the river, like one spoken of in yesterday's travel. One of the forks leads by Salmon Trout [Truckee] north, the southern by Carson's River. We took the latter, crossed a low elevation, and entered a similar flat which surrounds the sink, south, west, & north. To our left a little is a rich growth of maiden cane where the last of the river enters the sand. There are holes dug here for water but it is salt & stagnant and so not fit for use. Some of the train who intended to take in water here were disappointed, and all of us were in not being able to water the teams before starting across the desert stretch. Moving on, we now entered fairly the desert. A couple of miles brought us to some pools of water, which were not good, so we moved on a mile to a slough that Taplin thought better water. When we came to the pools Taplin was there with a horse and mule he had found The horse so much resembled "Charley," who was stolen from him, that all were fooled, and Taplin himself only knew the difference by a [sore wen ?] on Charley which this one had not. Mounting the mule he rode him to the lagoon where he was met by a man who was returning for them. This man was with a wagon which had gone on ten miles, into the desert, and having started across without grass or water, were debating whether to go on or turn back to procure grass and water and enter anew upon the dry stretch.[42] We watered our cattle from the slough which looked tolerable clear, although you could count 13 head of dead cattle decaying in it. When dipped up it looked like diluted lye, being colored with alkali. To neutralize this we put several tablespoons full of vinegar into each bucket full of water.[43] Having taken a cold lunch of bacon and bread, boiled rice, and stewed apples the Colonel & Taplin, provided with buffalo rugs, blankets, & provisions, started through to the river with the horses. Resting two hours the train was again "under way," Campbell's team going ahead with Griffith and Cockerill. Not far on we passed it, one of the oxen being down and they unable to get him up, Major Bassett standing by "looking like patience on a monument." The Dutch are behind, we fear in similar plight. Alex is still unable to ride horseback and we are very uneasy. It is impossible for Campbell's team to get through And we concluded if Griffith, who came from the same town with him, would not take him, we would, and haul him while we had an ox. At sundown Griffith & Cockerill stopt. They were a little before us. When we came up, not wishing to stop so early, we drove on until dark, some two miles farther. All concert of movement was now thrown aside, each one for himself driving as he thought best for his cattle. We intended to move again when the moon rose which would be about half past nine. Having our bread ready cooked and water being too precious to make coffee, we soon eat supper & having fed some of the hay to the cattle we went to bed in the wagon. Being very uneasy about Alex I got up, and Mr. Howard & myself started back to see in what condition he was. Just as we started Mr. Campbell met us having come up to see about getting Alex over. We told him that we would haul him, & that he must send Black Alex to wait on him. Soon after we passed Griffith, Campbell came up with him and although they had not spoke to each other for some time, having had a difficulty, this was lain aside, all ceremony waived. Having told Jack & Griffith that he could not get any farther with his cart, they took a yoke of their own cattle and got one from Cockerill & brought the cart up to their camp, and Griffith took Alex in his wagon, leaving Campbell packing. Campbell had passed the Germans who had drove by him when their steer laid down; and found them packing, Soon after starting from our noon halt, the boys (Howard's & Brown's wagon) had to take out an ox that was sick. They drove him along some time. I delayed a while at Campbell's wagon, and on coming up again, says Dock, "We are rescuing old Doc (the name of the ox)." He was cutting off his tail and ears to bleed him & also bleed him in the mouth. But all would not do; his "earthly career was over" and they had to leave him in the desert There was little sleeping done tonight, for the boys had scarce got to sleep when the moon appeared, our signal for moving. In a few minutes we were on our way. Griffith & Cockerill had just drove up and were again before us. A few miles on we saw a light as the fire of some campers; on coming up we found two men with a note from the Colonel, the purport of which was that the bearer, Mr. Owens, would pilot us around a hill and some heavy sand, for which we must haul some light bundles of clothes for his wife until we met his cart coming back. Here were half a dozen wagons left. Leading us off to the left about a hundred yards, down in a flat were some pools of water, holes dug about 6 feet, but strongly impregnated with alkali, so that we would not let our cattle drink of it. Traveling on five miles we came to where Owens had left his wagon and much of the load. Taking in the bundles we were to haul, we again started. Here one of Griffith's steers gave out, & we had to take Alex into our wagon, leaving Griffith. Thompson also stopped, his oxen having given out. We were now continually passing wagons and remains of wagons. About three o'clock we began to look out for wood to camp by. We had not gone far when we came to a wagon which made an excellent fire. It is the only sort of wood burnt in this desert, unless it is trunks, which are left in abundance. We fed the cattle some hay, and made some slapjacks, eat supper or early breakfast, and were soon trying to sleep, Tyle in the wagon and Nels & myself on a rug by the fire, with a blanket over each of us. But we were too cold to sleep well. Some distance back was a wagon, and on some planks was piled up 5 or eight hundred pounds of flour, with a note, saying "Gentlemen emigrants, this is tried flour and good; help yourselves," signed by Jones, who started with flour, bacon, &c. to

The Forty-Mile Desert.

Alkali Flats in the Forty-Mile Desert.

speculate on in California. We helped ourselves to one hundred pounds, which proved first rate.

This is truly a desert. There is not one spear of grass. Greasewood alone grows here. It is interspersed over the dry sand in bunches, or bushes, a few feet apart. It is singular from whence it receives nourishment, for it seldom rains here and no dew fall at this season of the year. Over the sand this evening was scattered a layer of scoriatic volcanic gravel, and stones. We passed also through a strange piece of country this evening. It was covered with sand hillocks from the size of potato hills to that of a mound for flowers—as the fellow said of the stone that was as large as a piece of chalk—fifteen feet in diameter and four or five high, these decked with greasewood as the rest of the country.

Late last evening we came to a slough strongly impregnated & colored with alkali, and along it a narrow strip of salt grass But around were lying divers dead oxen, warning future oxen "beware the tempting bait."

The road has been tolerable good, except now & then a little heavy sand. But the cattle are weak for want of water & from scant food. Old Pat has been sick all day and is given out as "past redemption."

. . . . .

SATURDAY, OCTOBER 6, 1849.

Dawn of day found us again on our weary way, Cockerill before. Soon he had gained a mile or two. His load is light and his cattle fresher and in better condition than ours. About ten o'clock we stopt, fried some meat, and took breakfast. We gave the cattle water here, what was in the cask, and threw the cask away, also a yoke which we had carried since leaving the cart so as to hitch an extra yoke on in an emergency, besides seven other articles to lighten our load. From here we could see Cockerill two miles off breakfasting on the top of a hill, the commencement of what [is] called the Ten Miles Stretch of Sand, as we learned from one of the Dutch who camped with us several nights ago, and who met us here. He was going back to assist a brother Dutchman who we met a few miles back, with his pack on a horse too poor to live and which he had driven until it would move no farther. Mr. Thomas passed on by us having rested and watered his cattle a mile back. After a half hour's stop we moved on again. When we came to the sand we found it would be impossible to get both our wagons to the river with the teams attached and so concluded to attach both teams to one waggon and roll through today and come back tomorrow evening and move the other through tomorrow night. Cockerill has moved on. Thomas & Barnes were going to rest here until 3 o'clock and then try to move through. Tyle, Mr. Howard, Dick and Horse, and Nelse went on with our wagon and all the cattle, leaving Dr. White, Brown, & myself to guard their wagon. We now had time to look around at the destruction. There were several wagons and a large lot of fine bacon. Several trunks lying about—Mr. Barnes had left a fine one and a large looking glass in a frame—and divers guns. Mr. Thomas left a double-barrel shotgun, & Frank (a German with him) had left a fine rifle; besides these were numerous articles, clothing, a canister of lamp oil, &c., all which they piled up and burnt.

About twelve o'clock Dent's team came up with 3 yoke of cattle and one following, two had given out & were left. After some consultation and deliberation, they concluded to leave their wagon and pack through. Going to work, they had packed their oxen and were ready to move by half past 3. Thompson had also arrived with two yoke attached to a cart and a loose steer following. About sundown Griffith came up with two yoke to a cart, his other yoke following. Last night they worked all night fixing a cart out of the hind wheels of a wagon with the fore axle [till?] & tongue. While talking with Griffith we were astonished to see Mr. Barnes coming back. He had drove a mile and could get no farther, and so sent Wallace on with the team and his wife and daughter walking through, and said Thompson had got that far on & was packing. Griffith & Johnston now determined to go on that far & pack. Barnes had come back to get one of us to go with him to guard his wagon. I accompanied him. Where he had stopt were several wagons left, one a large heavy wagon left by Jones. It had several hundred pounds of bacon in it. Thompson & Griffith & Johnson fell to work packing. Grif having thrown out a box of candles, they illuminated the camp, shedding a bright light to pack by. I retired to rest in Barnes' wagon, early. About ten o'clock I heard Alex asking for water. He was suffering. Campbell and his mess were back at our wagon and had sent Alex over to get a little water. Thompson had saved some that he had to water his steers, and furnished him with a canteen full. When I left the boys they had about a quart of water which they divided & drank up. In about an hour I heard Dr. Brown asking, "Can you give me a drink, gentlemen?" so thirsty he could scarce speak at all. Not long after Kapleman, Eilett, & Kramm came in, in the same condition.

About four o'clock Thompson, Griffith, and Johnson got off. Besides packing the cart, Thompson had packed Wash with two bundles of provisions. The poor fellow had more than he could get along with. Johnson, having compassion on him, tried to get him to leave one, but Wash would not. "Well," says Jack, "Give me one to carry through for you." Jack getting the bundle, him & Griffith eat what they wished & left it, and when they got through and Wash asked for the bundle Jack told him to tell Thompson he had left it.

· · · · ·

SUNDAY, OCTOBER 7, 1849.

Traveled by two o'clock at night since the morning of the 5th 47 miles. I rose this morning late. On looking around, the destruction of property here was greater than at any other one place. Here were a half dozen wagons & carts. One of the wagons was one left by Jones with perhaps a thousand weight of bacon in it. Thompson and Griffith had left divers articles, some of value, among them a fine glass inkstand, steel pens and a gold pen, a fine cloth coat never worn, and a case of surgical instruments—a common article of Thompson's.

While taking breakfast with Barnes, off of some excellent Boston crackers of Thompson's, and broiled bacon from Jones' wagon, Brown & White came over to get some water, being out. We had accidentally found a keg left by Thompson with a half gallon in it, & also a couple of boxes of soda powders on which we luxuriated. By ten o'clock, having returned to our wagon, we had finished the water. About this time Nelse came in sight with the mule loaded with water, having several gallons. We spent the rest of the day in reading and sleeping. About eight o'clock at night, Tyle & Humphreys came back with the oxen. We attached them to the wagon and were ready to move in an hour. So tedious a drive I never had before. When we came over to where Judge Barnes was, we found Taplin— who came that far with the boys—helping him to pack his goods & chattels into Griffith's cart, which they intended to take to the river where was a lighter one than his own, which Barnes intended to take possession of. Seven miles from the river we met John [Wilms?] coming back for an ox of his that was not yet through. We left him to sleep in the desert and hunt his ox when it was light. Some of us, walking forward, came across an ox of Campbell's, which we drove to the river. When he got there he was so thirsty that he rushed over a bank and fell with his head in the water & drank until his head went under & he drowned. Here was Campbell's [two words illegible] his saddle, the pony being lost in the willows. Going three miles up the river, we arrived at camp about one o'clock and soon had the cattle turned out and were asleep.

· · · · ·

MONDAY, OCTOBER 8, 1849.
MOVED 2 MILES.

Today was a busy day in camp. There was only four wagons got through. Barnes took possession of a wagon stood near camp, and which was lighter than his own. The rest of the company were packing, except Thompson took the cart Barnes brought through and was fixing his load in it. Thomas, who went a mile farther than we did, moved on this morning and Cockerill with him.

We unloaded and threw away some tools, soap, and little articles of not much value. The boys were busy razeeing their wagon. They cut several feet off the end, and coupled it shorter and tightened up some.

We see our friends of the desert, Owens, who guided us round some sand. They prove to be part of the company who were at Green River when we arrived there after covering the 40 mile stretch and who moved on on Sunday leaving us in camp. They have one wagon, and Uncle John is along with his cart.

Campbell found his horse this morning & is packing him.

About 3 oclock the cattle were driven up, hitched up, or packed, and we moved 2 miles up the river to a pretty, grassy camp under the shade of some grand, old, spreading, cottonwood trees.[44] It is pleasant to see these trees after so long a time without seeing anything of the kind. They now present the varied appearance of autumn, being in the sere & yellow leaf. We left Thompson & Campbell back at the last camp, Thompson having sent a black boy—Wash, about 15 years old—with an ox back ten miles on the desert, to where he commenced packing and where he had left divers articles which Wash was to pack back to camp that night.

This delay in crossing the desert has caused some uneasiness about getting over the mountains, and all are now for pushing ahead. Taplin appears uneasy. Although he talks as if he was not, you can see from the way he assists, to hurry us off, that he is ill at ease. The horrid fate of the Donner party[45] is staring in the face of some of the company. We hope, though, to move on [safely?] through, and have little fear of it being otherwise.

Ragtown on the Carson River, where emigrants rested after their desert crossing.

The Diary of Hugh Brown Heiskell

. . . . .

TUESDAY, OCTOBER 9, 1849.
TRAVELED 10 MILES.

This morning Campbell came up. He says Wash came in last night about 11 o'clock carrying a bag of crackers on his back & some other articles. He had drove the ox until it gave out then packed the load in himself. Soon after, the ox came in. During the night Campbell's horse broke into the bag of crackers and was luxuriating on them. Hearing him, Campbell got up to see what was going on. While up he heard a noise in the bushes like some animal walking. Standing in breathless excitement and seeing it advance [he] fired away as if thinking it a wolf. From the howl set up immediately he found he had shot Mingo, his dog. The ball passed through his fore leg, shattering it very much. We all moved off this morning, leaving Campbell, who intended to wait until Thompson came up, who was going to bring Mingo up in his cart. And then Campbell was going to [pack ?] him on his pony. Bassett, John Campbell, & the black boys left grumbling at his folly in carrying the dog and saying they would not wait on him.

This morning, Dr. White, Humphreys, & Brown were shooting at a mark. White loaded his gun, and fired away without taking his ramrod out. The gun kicked him severely, bruising his nose; his ramrod was shivered against the trees.

Moving up 2 miles, the road left the river. We now entered heavy sand. The pack ox train moved off this morning & the wagons could not keep up with them.

About 7 miles from where the road left the river it forked, the left leading immediately to the river; the right, going straight forward, strikes the river farther on. We took the former & could see the pack ox men on the latter. A mile & a half brought us to the river. Here was a beautiful camp, under large, spreading cottonwood trees, a fine carpet of grass, golden colored, being ready for the scythe. The trains came in about half an hour before the sun went down having made only ten miles, but the road was so heavy, and the cattle had not got over their hard drive across the desert, & thus moved slow.

About dark three men came riding up from the west, which we of course were glad to see to get news from California. They proved to be part of a relief company sent by General Smith to assist the emigrants across the mountains, for which purpose he has appropriated $100,000.[46]

WEDNESDAY, OCTOBER 10, 1849.
TRAVELED 10 MILES.

Our three relief men took supper & staid with us last night. They say we should push on night and day to get over the mountain before the snow sets in. We told them of Rice [Royce] who we met on the desert, going back for grass & water, with his wife in company. Two of them went back this morning to assist them. The other two pushed on to overtake Mr. Chandler, captain of the relief, and took Major Bassett, who they furnished a horse with them. They also left John Campbell a horse & mule for Barnes and family also a mule for Taplin.

The road today was again heavy sand, leading off from the river; when we had dragged our slow course along some eight miles we turned the cattle out to graze on bunch grass. Hitching up again we arrived at camp on the river two miles farther on, about two hours before sundown. One of the loose steers with our wagon fell behind & was not forthcoming this evening. Tyle rode back five or six miles to hunt him and returned at dark without success.

. . . . .

THURSDAY, OCTOBER 11, 1849.
TRAVELED 17 MILES.

Camp was up unusually early this morning. Perhaps these relief men urging us to push on had some effect. Tyle & Hanse, having breakfasted before it was light, started back for the ox left on yesterday. We lightened up again this morning. Threw away half our bacon, all our picks & shovels and Nelse his trunk. The boys threw away their trunks. Frank and myself were on cattle guard this morning, part of the cattle being on an island opposite camp, part across the river, and next to camp in the willows, [they] were hard to collect. We finally got them all but one of ours, but made a late start. I remained behind to hunt the missing steer, and wading the river found him among the reeds in fine pasture.

Six miles from camp we crossed the river and moved one mile & a half above. Had fried ham & pickles for dinner.

Tyle and myself were on guard until eleven. The night was clear & cold. While on guard we heard the Colonel's horse neigh below camp, he having got loose from where he was tied. We were a little uneasy for fear he should go back again, but did not find him.

· · · · ·

FRIDAY, OCTOBER 12, 1849.
TRAVELED ———— MILES.

The Colonel rode the mare down among the willows to hunt his horse, and as the train started, we heard him call Tyle to help him, as the mare was mired. Moving six miles, we nooned where the road crossed the river. Tyle came up packing my saddle, "as mad as a wet hen" that we had left it. Colonel also gave up the hunt for his horse and overtook us here.

It was now about 11 o'clock. We set to work cutting grass & baking bread, as we intended to move through the 12 mile stretch round the canyon By 2 o'clock we were again on the way. Having crossed the river—here about 40 feet wide & two deep—we moved on 7 miles & camped in a grove of shrubby cedar, without water or grass. We fed the cattle of the grass we had cut, eat a cold supper, without coffee, for we had no water to make coffee of, and enjoyed ourselves sitting by a large blazing fire of dead & dry cedar.

· · · · ·

SATURDAY, OCTOBER 13, 1849.
TRAVELED 15 MILES.

Morning clear and cold. As we had the cattle tied up and little cooking to do, we got off early. Five miles brought us to the river. Here we found our friend Edwards, who took Bassett on. He had with him two other men, and several mules, and was waiting to assist us through. They persuaded Barnes to pack through with his wife and daughter, giving them a mule each to ride. Taplin gave up the one he had rode. Wallace [Barnes] was left to drive the wagon through. There was also a mule left for Alex, who is able to walk a little and will soon we hope be able to ride. While taking lunch here Captain Clayton came up with several others. He left the States with Sackett,[47] who he left on Mary's River with his wife and a carriage with mules attached. Clayton has fallen in with Remington, and they are packing. Having hitched up, as we left Thomas was before & took the wrong road, thus our team got before him, but he drove in before the boys. Doc requested him not to drive in between us as we messed together & had drove together ever since we left St Jo. Says Thomas: "I have a right to drive here." "Well," says Doc, "I'll drive your team out." "If you do," returned Thomas, "I shall hit you." A disagreeable but [funny?] rumpus now ensued. Doc drove the oxen out of the road &

Thomas struck him a severe blow on the head with his whipstock, cutting it somewhat. Doc now downed him. The old lady was flying round getting in to the [illegible word] of every one near, crying, "Murder! They will murder him. You are all a set of murderers." But the boys kept her from interfering, and although she pulled their hair & slapped them, through respect to the sex no one struck her. While Doc had Thomas down, says Brown: "Doc, give him a little, but don't hurt him." "Ah," says Dick, "Give him hell, by jolly, give him hell." "No," replied Doc, "I don't want to hurt him," & let him up. Thomas now drove his team out, of his own accord.

. . . . .

SUNDAY, OCTOBER 14, 1849.
IN CAMP.

Again we have a day of rest, but we must acknowledge that it was as much policy as piety that induced us to lay by, for now it is "dangerous to delay." But we thought that with one day's rest the cattle would take us out of danger sooner than if we traveled on.

Our relief friends, with Barnes & family, camped with us last night & left this morning. While at breakfast, Nichols & Paine came up, who went back to assist Rice [Royce], who we left going back on the desert. They gave him some mules and left him with them packed and his oxen.

There was two oxen missing today—one of Cockerill's & one of Wallace's. The Indian fires are seen all around us burning on the mountain side, and Doc & Hanse saw one wading the creek in a state of nudity, spearing fish. He had killed two fine ones which he gave to Doc, who gave him in return an old pair of pants. We had fine bean soup for dinner and fish. Brown, our best soup maker, was cook. This, our regular Sunday dish, we have missed for two previous Sunday[s] as we traveled.

We read some in the "book divine" today, but were principally engaged in bringing up journals, with ["which" omitted?] we were behind since crossing the desert, as there was not time then for writing.

MONDAY, OCTOBER 15, 1849.
TRAVELED 18 MILES.

Morning very cold. The two missing oxen were not found this morning. It is supposed that an Indian drove them off. We moved from this fine grassy spot, about 8 o'clock. We are now in one of the most beautiful ["spots" omitted?] in the world. For 25 miles to the southwest is stretched out a level plain, & on your left 15 or 20 miles, bounded on all sides with mountains. We see, on west of us a day's journey, some skifts of snow on the top of a peak of the range along whose base we are now traveling. The whole side of that mountain presents a white appearance which we would take for snow, if it was not for the contrast between it and the pure snow near its summit.[48] Behind these hills we now & then have a view of the Sierra Nevada. During the day, every few hundred yards brought us to a bold, clear running ["stream" omitted?], cold as if immediately from the snow. Just before nooning, and about 8 miles from camp, we passed along the immediate base of the mountains where by the side of the road, boil out a thousand hot springs, forming a large lagoon covered with rushes, ["making" omitted?] its way slowly to the river. From the springs rise a strong ["odor" omitted?] of carburetted hydrogen.[49] A mile farther on we nooned at one of the numerous rills rippling down into the valley.

Seven miles this evening brought us to the white mountain spoken of above. The ridge for several miles here presents a white appearance, but this is a prominent part of it, rising a thousand feet above the valley. It is composed of granite, which seems to be crumbled off yearly by the freezes, making gravel & small rock which lodge in the crevices & sides of the hill. Among the rock are interspersed pine trees, as the rest of the chain has been today. About camp were found several skulls, supposed to be of Indians.

Tonight we have the pleasure of sitting by a large fire made of pine logs, which gratifies us after so long having nothing but willow bushes.

· · · · ·

TUESDAY, OCTOBER 16, 1849.
TRAVELED 12 MILES.

Morning cool, but midday quite warm. We continued crossing streams every few hundred yards as yesterday. We passed a grove of cottonwood & pine to our left with one of these streams running through it. Having traveled eight miles, we came to where the river canyons; descending a hill we nooned at a spring with a green plot of meadow land around it.

Starting about half past two we entered a grove of noble pines some [of] which we noticed were 8 feet in diameter—yellow pine, but the leaf is a little longer than ours and the limbs put out near the ground. The hills now closed in & we entered the canyon. On each side mountains of granite raise their rugged summits a thousand feet above us; among the craggy rock are growing pines to their tops. There is a pass left for the river—here a roaring creek. This pass is a narrow gorge covered with majestic pines, upon which the hills have encroached, by the rolling down from their sides and summit large boulders of rock and thousands of smaller rock. These have impeded the course of the stream & made this the roughest road ever wagons were driven over. The rock are loosened I suppose by hard freezing, and when thawed again roll down. We have been ascending rapidly, the four miles which we came this evening. Crossed the river twice, and camped in the canyon after a strenuous effort to get through and late drive. To drive with any sort of safety required two hands. Wallace, who was by himself turned his wagon over, which delayed us a few minutes, but we unloaded it & turned it back almost as quick as it was capsized. Wagons have paid a heavy tribute through this pass. Broken axletrees, wheels, beds, and all the parts of a wagon scattered along the road. I noticed 9 wheels or rims of wheels at our camp.

It was warm today and there were scattering white clouds & a south wind blowing. Some of the boys were uneasy for fear it would rain and snow, but the wind shifted, & as we lay down to rest we could ["hear it" omitted?] roaring through the trees from the north, which calmed their fears.

. . . .
The Carson River Gorge at the foot of the Sierra.

The Diary of Hugh Brown Heiskell

WEDNESDAY, OCTOBER 17, 1849.
TRAVELED 12 MILES.

This morning the wind was blowing from the north and quite cold. The stars shone bright until lost in the blaze of day. The sun was late making his appearance, being hid by the hills, but finally shone out clear & with autumnal brightness.

We packed the mule left for Alex & the mare, & the boys packed our mule. Thus lightened we moved on this morning & found the road worse even than yesterday. A regular wagon driver would have thrown up his hands in despair and pronounced it impassable. But we move on as there was no possible retreat. The steers would lose footing and fall & perhaps be hauled along on the rocks some distance before we could stop the team. While crossing the creek—a most rugged ford and dangerous drive—Brown & Nelse were just over. They were driving the pack horses & oxen, and amid the uproar of the dashing stream & drivers hollering and wagon ripping over rocks, Brown struck at an ox to make him go on & his gun went off & came near shooting him. About ten o'clock we once more got into the "open air." The gorge, having gradually widened here two miles from camp, formed a valley with grass for the cattle where we nooned. A few hundred yards back we met Frank, who was looking for John Campbell's horse. Our company who left us Sunday having camped here last night, he was not found this morning As we came in we saw the horse grazing among the willows and called Frank back.

This evening we traveled 10 miles, still ascending & approaching a spur of the Sierra Nevada with snow along its sides. Just before camping we came to where there was snow by the side of the road. Our camp was at Red Lake, the head of

Red Lake from Carson's Pass.
The thick reed growth shows at
lower left.

Carson's River. It is a small sheet of water surrounded with mountains, and it appears to be encroached upon by the flags, for they cover half its surface. This we cut for the oxen. Tyle & Brown waded in on the turf formed by the flags—water among them two feet deep; now & then their feet would sink through the turf into the lake underneath.

. . . . .

Thursday, October 18, 1849.
Traveled 7 miles.

Having packed the loose animals, we commenced the ascent of the Sierra Nevada. It was very steep & rocky, for a mile and a half. Having belabored each team and made half the ascent, we found it impossible to make the summit, and doubled teams. Then with much labor—setting wheels, cracking whips, & hallooing—we dragged our slow course along.[50] Having reached the top we descended to Lake Valley 3 1/2 miles, which lies between the ridge we crossed this morning and another at whose base it lies, which is the last of the mountain. There are two lakes in the valley, one several feet above the other, separated by a narrow neck of land covered with trees. Each several hundred yards in diameter. They are supplied with water by clear small streams from the snow, which is reflected in the bosom of the lake perpetually, where it has lodged in the ravines or crevices of the mountains to the east, south, & west. North of the lake, where the sun strikes the south side of the mountain, there is no snow.

As we descended the mountain this morning, we were met by our friend Edwards & Nichols of the relief party. They brought us 6 yoke of cattle to assist

. . . .

The last hundred yards of the emigrant trail below Carson's Pass.

The Diary of Hugh Brown Heiskell

us. We could have [managed?] without danger, but we will not insult Uncle Sam by refusing his aid.[51] We encamped about 11 o'clock & turned our cattle on good grass. During the evening, while chatting round a fire, our attention was called to a bell ringing, & descending the mountain from the west soon a pack train came in sight. It proved to be another relief party of which Hunt[52] was captain—a man who passed with us from St. Louis up the Missouri on the <u>Timour</u>. They are going pack as far as the desert to assist all the needy. Our pack train are getting on well as they are in 3 days of Sutter's. Thomas & Thompson were on the top of the mountain as they came on. Hunt's account of the mines are cheering.

A government train came in during the evening, from the States. An escort with Captain Johnson, Sub Indian Agent of California. He left General Wilson on Mary's River, who is the Agent.[53]

Soon after Johnson arrived, Rice [Royce] came in with his oxen packed and his wife riding a mule—furnished them by Uncle Sam—& carrying a child. Among his cattle, as they drove them up we noticed the oxen lost by Wallace & Cockerill last Sunday. On making enquiry about them and telling him that they belonged to them, he replied that he had bought them from a fellow who found them for 20 dollars & they could be had for 25. Wallace & Cockerill came back to see what was to be done, & Taplin went to see Rice. On his telling him he had paid twenty dollars and they could not be got until he, Rice, was paid that much, Taplin told the boys to drive the cattle up with the rest of ours, & told Rice to come up to camp & he would give him his note for 20 dollars. There is a Dutchman with Rice who was shot on Salmon Trout River (or Carson's). He belong[ed] to the unfortunate train that lost their cattle on the Hasting's Cutoff, and are straggling in small parties or singly. He was by himself. Three Indians attacked him. An arrow entered his left breast a short distance. He shot at one, wounded one of them. The others bore him off & escaped. His wound is slight.

. . . . .

FRIDAY, OCTOBER 19, 1849.
TRAVELED 12 MILES.

We had determined to make an early start this morning, & so camp was astir sooner than common. But on driving up the cattle, the government oxen were not with them so we were delayed until 8 o'clock. Then we commenced the toilsome ascent of the last & highest ridge of the Sierra. It was five miles to the sum-

The Diary of Hugh Brown Heiskell

mit, most of the way very steep, though it is descending in some places, and at one time we descended rapidly several hundred yards. About 1 o'clock we reached the summit, where we found a fire ready for cooking, with a kettle of snow on melting to make coffee with. While it was boiling we found a little stream trickling down from the snow melting at the top. As we ascended there was a bank of [snow] on our left 15 or 20 feet deep, and crossed streams of water from the melting snow. On the side of the mountain is a camp where Dr. Brown of St. Louis was caught in a snow storm the 10 of Oct. His horses and cattle were frozen to death, their carcases lying round, & the remains of a wagon. He himself & wife moved on in the snow several feet deep, but were relieved by government mules.

The mountainside this morning was covered with spruce pine and beautiful grass growing among them on the benches, the top bare of vegetation.

The descent was rapid, and we pushed on late to come up with Edwards & Nichols, who said when they left us they intended to make Chandler's camp, but fell short of them and camped in rock valley at a little stream with scarcely any grass for the cattle. We turned them loose to pick a scant supper & tied them up at nine o'clock.

As we came down the mountain, we found John Campbell lying by the side of the road, his horse dead by him. He had fallen behind Thomas, & his horse could not keep up. They went on without sending back to see what had become of him, with his provisions, leaving him—who is so affected in his legs that he cannot walk—to the mercy of the Indians and Sierra Nevada, or the doubtful tender mercies of the emigrants behind. We placed him in Wallace's wagon and moved on to camp.

. . . . .

SATURDAY, OCTOBER 20, 1849.
TRAVELED 12 MILES.

Morning as usual cold, but for some days the weather has been quite pleasant.

Before the sun was up we were again on our weary way; in search of grass This we found 8 miles from camp, where we arrived about 11 o'clock and turned our cattle a half mile to the right of the road on excellent bunch grass. Last year at this spring three Mormons were killed by Indians and are buried in one grave near the spring.

Moving on at one o'clock a mile, we found a quantity of provisions—flour, rice, crackers, meat, &c.,—left by Uncle Sam for the needy emigrants. We, not coming under that head, did not take any. There was a few pounds of flour & crackers put in for Campbell, who certainly is needy. Rice, who was out of flour, was helping himself. And our Dutchman who was shot on Carson's River helped himself greedily.

Two miles from "Provision Rock," we found grass to the left of the road a few hundred yards, in a deep hollow, where was a fine little spring. Here Johnson had encamped. We have seldom so much rejoiced as this evening on finding such excellent grass, that we might rest our cattle and ourselves on the Sabbath morrow, for without grass—what we expected—of course we would again have had to encroach upon this day of rest. We spread our tents on the grass & spent the evening till bed time in social commerce round a log fire, then retired to sleep in peace, leaving Mr. Howard on guard and Campbell asleep before the fire. About twelve in the night we were aroused by Mr. Howard shouting, "Boys! boys! Here! here! The Indians have shot an arrow into John. Run, get your guns." Such confusion as there now was has seldom ever been seen. We all rushed out not half awake in our "night apparel" enquiring "What is the matter?" & running to the wagons for the guns. The confusion subsiding, the guard was doubled, & keeping a vigilant watch we were not again troubled. At the time of the shooting Mr. Howard was sitting by the fire & hearing John hollow, on looking round the arrow was quivering in him.

[The camp that night provided accommodation for a heterogeneous group: the remnants of the Bicknell train—the two Monroe mess wagons, the Cockerill wagon and the Barnes wagon; a detachment of soldiers who were accompanying Captain Johnson to his post; several individual travelers; and Mr. and Mrs. Josiah Royce and their daughter Mary. The whole group traveled together with other single travelers on the 18th, 19th, and 20th of October.

Sarah Bayliss Royce gave an account of the Indian attack similar to Hugh Heiskell's, but briefer.

On the night of October 21st we unloaded our packs and made our fires within a few rods of our courteous protectors. We had, as usual, made for our own little family a sort of barricade of packs somewhat retired from the others; the men were lying near their fire asleep; and all was still; when a sudden, loud outcry, as of mingled pain and fright followed by other hasty exclamations, and rushing footsteps, and, soon, two or three shots roused us all. We were quickly informed that two Indian arrows had been fired into our neighbors' camp, evidently aimed at the men who were sleeping in the light of their fire. One of the arrows had wounded a man, striking him directly on one of the large ribs, which had prevented its reaching the vitals. The other arrow missing its aim and fell on the ground. Several of the men rushed, armed, into the thicket whence the arrows came, fired, and pursued a short distance . . . . The wounded man proved not to be mortally wounded; and we had the satisfaction of knowing he was improving before we finally parted company—which occurred a day or two later.][54]

. . . . .

SUNDAY, OCTOBER 21, 1849.
TRAVELED 15 MILES.

This morning we found the tracks of Indians in 30 steps of camp fire, and the arrow with which John was shot. It had gone through six ply of blankets with which he was covered, and three shirts, also his webbing belt, and penetrated his left side, stopping against the lower rib. We also found an arrow a few steps from the fire which we suppose was shot at Mr. Howard but passed him, as where it lay ranged with the direction from which the other was shot. These arrows are neat pieces of workmanship. In the first place is a well feathered arrow, of some straight sprout—willow, perhaps. The barb, which is a piece of thick glass, shaped as the common flint barb but smaller & keener, is fastened to a rod of very hard, tough timber 4 inches long. This rod is a little smaller than the rest of the arrow, & being sharpened is fitted in to a hole drilled in the end of the arrow with great skill, there secured by being neatly wrapped with the sinews of some animal.

From the hostility of the Indians, it was thought best to move on today, so about ten o'clock we left "Camp [Plum?]." About 3 miles from here we came to Leeks Spring. Here were 13 wagons, belonging to Jones, Dr. Brown of St Louis, & another company. The indians had driven off 30 head of their cattle & 20 mules of Jones, and a mule & horse belonging to some of the others. Jones had just heard from a party sent in pursuit of the cattle. They followed the trail on which the Indians took them 35 miles and came up with the cattle. One was dead, with an arrow sticking in him and the warm blood running out, several others were wounded—the mules & horse were shot. Jones' mules were driven another direction and six men in pursuit of them from whom there was no intelligence.

We moved on rapidly today and made 15 miles to Camp Creek by sundown. Here we found no grass, cut a few willow bushes for the cattle, & tied them to the wagon. Taplin caught a mule on the road going back, which was tied up.

Rice [Royce] came up and camped with us. Johnson went on seven miles farther.

Epilogue

· · · · ·

THE END OF THE JOURNEY

Hugh Heiskell's journal ends as abruptly as it begins, when he and his companions were starting down the western slope of the Sierra Nevada to the gold fields. What happened next must be pieced together from other sources.

During the last ten days of their journey, the Bicknell train moved up the West Fork of the Carson River to its source in Red Lake and then over the Sierra Nevada in two difficult days, the path generally followed by modern state Route 88. Three miles beyond Tragedy Spring the travelers turned their wagons north and west toward the headwaters of Camp Creek. A ridge between the north fork of the Cosumnes and the south fork of the American River led toward the gold fields. The tortuous way over the mountains completed the breakup of Colonel Bicknell's train. Those who were packing got ahead of the wagons, although they ran the risk of Indian attacks if they moved in small groups. Still, there remained some sense of association—in Hugh Heiskell's mind, at any rate—when, three days before he ceased keeping his diary, he picked up the ill John Campbell, who had been left behind on the roadside by his messmates. Forty-niners first came upon gold diggers at the confluence of Webber and Ringgold Creeks, at a settle-

· · · · · · · · · · · ·

Weaverville in 1849.

Webber Creek, 1995.

ment known as Weaverville or Webberville. The components of the Bicknell train straggled into the gold camp in disarray.

The governor of California, mindful of the fate of the Donner party three years earlier, tried to hasten the crossing of the last emigrants before the snows began by sending out relief parties along all the major emigrant routes. They provided food and in some cases riding or draft animals, which they distributed among the parties as they assessed their needs.[1] From the Bicknell company, for instance, Mr. and Mrs. Barnes and their daughter received government mules so that they could ride across the mountains, leaving Wallace Barnes to drive the last lap of the journey in the wagon they had commandeered on Carson River.

Sarah Royce, who helped keep a store in Weaverville set up by her husband in partnership with three miners, has related her experiences in the town in November and December of 1849. Their home was merely the curtained-off rear part of the double tent that served as a store, but she felt happy to be settled after the trials of the journey, though there were only two other women in the town, one of whom left early in November. Nearly all the dwellings that sprawled along Webber Creek were tents, with a few log cabins here and there. Sarah Royce and other observers that fall and winter noted the prevalence of illness among the emigrants, particularly cholera, scurvy, and diarrhea. "I know of companies of ten to fifteen men who crossed the plains," wrote Alonzo Delano, "everyone of whom were down sick at once, with no one to wait on them. Some recovered and some died."[2] Both the Royces fell ill, Josiah with cholera after a trip to Sacramento, and Sarah with a fever that left her bedridden. She had still not recovered fully when they moved south just after Christmas. Observers attributed the high incidence of sickness among emigrants to various causes: debility from the hardships of the journey across the plains; diet, particularly the lack of vegetables, which were scarce and dear even in California; extreme temperature and heavy rains; living in tents or under trees with inadequate covers; drinking river water; and poor personal hygiene.

The Monroe County nucleus of the Bicknell train were still acting together after the emigrants reached Weaverville. They had survived the crossing of the desert and the Sierra, and even an Indian raid, but now they faced new conditions and dangers of different kinds. The rainy season would soon begin, and the group split in two. Hugh Heiskell, the two Whites, Howard, and Cannon remained at Weaverville to start building a cabin, while Colonel Bicknell, Tyler Heiskell, Brown, and Humphreys went on to Sacramento to buy supplies for the winter. There they disposed of their extra wagon and stock, retaining one wagon to haul supplies. From the new city that was rising near the site of Sutter's Fort, Tyler Heiskell wrote to inform his father of their safe arrival in California.

Dear Father:

I am at last able to inform you of our arrival in California after a long, laborious, tedious, and tiresome journey, and all in good health, and without any loss of property. Col. Bicknell, Brown, Humphreys and myself are now in this city of a day, and Oliver and Dick White, Nelson Cannon, Hugh Heiskell, and Mr. Howard, are at this time on Weaver's Creek, near Weaversville, sixty miles east of this place. Our effects that we brought over are there, and we came down here to buy and haul up our winter provisions. It has been two weeks since we left them, but I received a note from Hugh a few days since, saying they were all well except Nelson, and he was improving or nearly well; he was a little sick when we left there. They think the prospect for making money is as good as any could wish.

We got to the first mines the 24th October, six months and eight days from the time we left home, and five months and one day from the time we left St. Joseph, Mo. I will not be able to give you a very satisfactory letter for want of time, talent, and a fire to write it by, but I could write a week and not tell half the prospect for making money. It is as great as the most loving of the "filthy lucre" could wish. I cannot say what I can make mining, for we have done nothing since we got through, and no man knows what he can average, but some make a hundred and fifty dollars per day for months, and others only sixteen. Any person will tell you that he can make one ounce any where. That the article is superabundant, I will prove by giving you a few of "the prices current," not quoted, but what I have seen and bought at—viz: Flour $32 per barrel—mess of pickled pork about $60 per barrel of 200 lbs.; Fresh Beef 25 cents per pound.; Salt Beef $20 per bbl. of 200 lbs.; Coffee 30 cts. per lb. by the Sack; Sugar, best article, 28 cts. by the bbl.; Onions $1 per lb.; Potatoes $1 per lb.; Apples $1.25 per doz.; Peaches $2 per lb.; a very small green cabbage head $4 each; Fish of the best kind, 50 cts. per lb.; Butter $1.50 per lb. by the hundred lbs.; Plank is worth $500 per thousand feet.

I find one College mate here, R. A. Paris of Tazewell county, Va., building a house of the plank, hewn from red wood (arbor vitae,) a plank six feet long, and six inches wide, which cost him 90 cts. each plank; Shingles $50 per thousand, and such as you would not let Riley put on a pig pen. Hauling $12 per hundred, for from 20 to 45 miles and over that to 60 miles $15. These are a few of the prices in this city of tents, and the prices doubled after being hauled 20 miles or more.

As to exhausting the gold in the mines, I think it will not be done in twenty years. It is found South of this place, 180 miles on the Sacramento, about the same distance North, and on every intermediate stream, and on almost every dry ravine. In traveling from Weavertown to this place, in nearly every hollow, I found persons mining, and the ravines have been dug up. Nearly every oak afforded a company of miners a house, thousands have no other house but the oak, and their blankets, and in this country up to this time they render a man comfortable, but now the rainy season has set in, they will have to leave these diggins [*sic*]; i. e. those in the wet diggins will have to leave, and come to the dry.

This city is on the Sacramento, 140 miles above San Francisco, and six months ago there was not a house here, and now the population is estimated at ten thousand. Most of the houses are canvass, many tents, no good building. The best in the city is the City Hotel, which cost one hundred and twenty thousand dollars, and it could be put up in Madisonville for three thousand dollars, and that is extravagant.

This place supplies all the miners North of this, half of the mining districts. The river is navigable for large Steam Ships up to this place, and there are now lying at the levee fifty or sixty Crafts, of all kinds, Sloops, Schooners, &c., yet it is in the woods and will soon be in the water. My old College mate, Dr. R. A. Paine, got here in September last, and has made nine or ten thousand dollars, buying and selling Town Property, Physician, and Druggist. He pays his clerk $300 per month.

And I also met long John M. Barnes, formerly from Blount County, Tennessee, who now lives in Oregon. He got to the mines, or commenced mining the 4th August last, and to the last of October, dug twenty-five hundred dollars. I saw the gold, no mistake about his "dust." He was the happiest man I ever saw, in his gold, and meeting us, but his gold most.— He could hardly contain himself; "a soul redeemed from a load of guilt" at a Camp Meeting never cut as many extras as did he. He says that he was extremely poor when he left home, and has gone back to make his family comfortable; for his friends I will say, that his children are all alive and well. He let his wheat crop fall and rot, and most of the Oregon people did the same. The young Keans live near him and doing well, one of them came to California with him, but was sick and made nothing. Frank Smith is at Weaverville, I see his name on a ticket to represent that district in the first California Legislature, which takes place on the 16th inst. Old Capt. Sutter, long a resident of California, the owner of this land, is a candidate for Governor, opposed by Winfield Scott Sherwood. I know nothing about the probable success of either.

The convention assembled, some time since, and formed a Constitution, which is submitted to the people at the coming election, for adoption or rejection. I know but one clause and that is, that Slavery or involuntary servitude, shall not exist in California. This State has no use for a Congress to decide that question, for that will be the law of the land, whenever the State is fully organised, if left to the people to decide. Every man who in the States was entitled to vote, can vote here, and some of the natives, but I do not know the qualifications for a native. This is a bad place to get information of any kind; no newspapers, nor will any person talk to you unless you give him $1 per hour. Time is money. I have seen but one newspaper since I got to the place, the N. York Herald, September 4th, from which I suppose Trousdale is elected Governor of Tennessee, and some person told me Crozier was beaten for Congress by a Whig—Col. Jo. Anderson.

I hope we will have the general result, and letters from home, on Col. Bicknell's return, who is now in San Francisco.

Capt. Sutter is a fine looking, honest Dutchman, liberal and kind, good hard sense, and is now here electioneering, like a Tennessee Sheriff whose time has expired, but a candidate for re-election. He says "that he has governed Indians, Spaniards and white men, and if they will elect him Governor they will say old Jno. A. Sutter is a pretty good Governor." There is some sickness here, and it would be impossible to be otherwise, people living out of doors, under trees and in tents. We will go back to where we left the "boys," build us a cabin, and live comfortable during the Winter or wet season. Wood is worth from sixteen to twenty dollars per cord, pine plank, (very scarce) 25 cents per pound. You pay for every thing here. If you look a man rather strait, he charges you a dollar, and I have not been so extravagant as to look at a "gal," yet in this place. Where there are supposed to be ten thousand souls, there are not more than fifty women. This is a fine market for them, and if the lady from New York would come with her ship load I vouch for her a fortune.—I paid 50 cts. for the privilege of grinding two axes, hold my self and furnish the turner.—No person considers the prices high here, and indeed they are not, considering the price of labor. An ox driver gets $10 per day, and a mechanic from sixteen to twenty. Gambling is carried to a greater extent than any place I ever heard of before— no public house but what is filled with gaming tables. They cannot be avoided by any person who wishes to do so, and with them a bar, but for all this, there was never better order in any village of the States. I have been here a week and a half and have not seen three drunken men. You are treated like a gentleman, you hear no hallooing in the town nor around it. several churches well attended, still there is no Sabbath here, work and gaiming [sic] the same every day. The owners of slaves have no difficulty in retaining and receiving their services. There is a fortune here for every man in California.—There is one for me and if I keep my health I will make it, and not be always about it either, and come home. I wish some of the other friends were here, and if any of them do come, or any person, I can give them some information, that would do them good service.—Do not cross the plains; 'tis too long, tedious and toilsome a trip, but if they do cross, use pack mules, for if they start with a wagon, they will in all probability lose their teams. We left St. Josephs, Mo., a company of twelve wagons. We got to the sink of Mary's river, 1800 miles from St. Josephs, with 10 wagons, the teams very weak. From Mary's to Barson's [*sic*] river, a distance of 39 miles, there is not a vestige of vegetation seen nor a drop of water, but a few salt wells dug by the emigrants, and the water not fit to use. After letting our cattle rest a day, cutting and curing grass, our casks filled with water, we took the desert, and but five wagons got through. Mr. Campbell's (a brother of Jas. W. of Knoxville,) mess lost five oxen, their wagon, their clothing and provisions, but what they could pack on their backs and one steer. A second mess well provided with every thing, and a Doctor with a fine stock of medicines, lost five head of cattle, their wagon, much fine and laborers clothing, got through with an ox and cow packed and what they had on their backs.—A third mess lost four oxen, out of eight, a wagon and a firstrate outfit, getting what they could pack on four broken down oxen. A fourth mess lost three oxen out of six, and abandoned their outfit. A fifth, abandoned all but what they could pull in a cart with two poor steers. The sixth mess got a cart through, abandoning half their outfit. Three others got through, with great difficulty.—The other team was mules. The sand was 10 or 12 inches deep and that played the duce with our teams. We (Monroe boys,) doubled our teams at the sand, took one wagon through, rested a day, and brought the other very easy. Nor was the desert more disastrious [*sic*] to ours than to companies preceeding [*sic*] us. The last twenty-eight of the thirty-nine miles was one continued scene of destruction of property, horses, mules, oxen, wagons, provisions of all kinds, fine and common clothing, and every thing that man could think of for his comfort or use. The last fifteen miles would average a wagon for every two hundred yards, nor were we out of the stench of dead animals one step. A wagon load of bacon was left with the name of the owner, and his card telling all to help themselves. In another place about 1000 pounds of flour with the same card. These were the largest lost left, but thousands of pounds strewed the desert.

Soon after getting on Carson's river the emigrants were met by the government relief parties, with mules, oxen, and provisions, and just in time for many. We crossed one ridge of the mountains before any was offered to us, and we could of got through without any assistance, but we took a pair of Uncle Sam's oxen and got through with ease.

Gov. Smith deserves the gratitude of the emigrants for the assistance rendered them, many of whom would have suffered otherwise. I suppose he was acting under instructions from the President, still much credit is due him for the promptness and order in which the business was done. We were later crossing the plains than I would ever be again. On the 19th [10th?] October there was a snow storm before us, in which a Dr. Brown of St. Louis was caught—his horses and four steers were frozen to death. His wife suffered greatly walking in snow two and three feet deep. It had melted when we got there, but the roads were still covered with ice in many places, and much snow in banks on the sides of the mountains.

The Indians became very troublesome to the last part of the emigrants—killed and run off a great deal of stock. Mr. Campbell was shot with an arrow while sleeping by the fire at our tent. They had been trying to steal some mules from a government train and were shot at—this enraged them—they came by our camp, Campbell was sleeping and Corneli[u]s Howard was on guard, sitting by him. They were both shot at, but Howard was missed. The other being more skillful hit Campbell, the arrow penetrating six folds of heavy blanketing, a vest, three shirts, a webbing belt, lodged against the first long rib below. The camp was soon up, but not a gun was loaded nor did any person know where the ammunition was but in about two hours we were all ready for the fight, and then we all went to bed and slept soundly till day.

My letter is already too long, but I could not make it any shorter. I am in a tent—the wind blowing like thunder, and roaring like all the flood gates of heaven were drifted away—a tin pan turned over my knee and my paper resting upon it. "Nuff sed."

Your affectionate son
TYLER D. HEISKELL[3]

From Sacramento, Colonel Bicknell went to San Francisco to pick up mail for the group. He wrote home to apprise friends and relations of the successful completion of their journey:

Dear Brother:—After a very long, and (toward the last) very fatiguing journey, we have arrived safe and sound in the golden country, for which we ought to be thankful. We left the frontier at St. Joseph, Mo., on the 23d of May and arrived at the first diggings on the 24th of Oct., making the trip in five months and one day.

After leaving Fort Laramie and passing the South Pass, we followed Sublets cut-off instead of going by the Salt Lake, which I regret very much since we gained but little by it and missed seeing (as I have since learned by persons who came that route) one of the most beautiful and fertile spots on the globe, the Mormon city and settlements.

We met with no accident on the route, except the loss of horses, stolen by the Indians. On Mary's or Humboldt's river, Dr. Oliver White's horse was stolen; the night before Mr. Taplin lost his horse. We met with no more losses until we got across the desert, on Carson's river, where I lost my fine Spanish horse, that I bought near Laramie, he was taken by the whites or Indians, and I do not know which.

After we cross[ed] the Sierra Nevada (pronounced here the Seara Navetha) the Indians shot an arrow at a man who was lying by our fire, the arrow went through six folds of his blanket, through his coat, vest, pants, three shirts and a belt and lodge against his lower rib; it was very painful for a day or two, but Dr. White soon set it all right.

We crossed the mountain on the 19th of October and on the 30th it was blocked up with snow. We have never traveled on Sabbath but once since we left the frontier, and then we had no grass for our cattle, and were compelled to move to where we could find some.

We arrived at Weaverton on Weaver creek, about fifty miles from Sutter's Fort, on the 24th Oct., and determined to winter there, and left our baggage, Dr. White, R. L. White, Mr. Howard, Nelson Cannon, and Hugh Heiskell to cut logs for building our cabins, and select a place for digging. Tyler Heiskell, John Brown, Andrew Humphreys and myself came on with the wagons to Sacramento city, on the Sacramento river, at Sutter's Fort, fifty miles, for the purpose of putting our cattle out to grass or selling them. I left the boys to attend to it, and came down to this city [San Francisco] to get letters, papers, &c. I paid for my passage down to this place $35, and now pay $6 per day for board. I have been here four days and have just succeeded in getting our letters. I received but one, that was yours of the 24th June. Hugh Heiskell has received his regular files from the time he left home; the rest of the boys have received nothing. I received two numbers of the Register for June. I have mailed several newspapers to our friends, which will give you all the news in the country. I shall vote for the constitution, I believe, and I think I shall vote for old Sutter for Governor.

Well, now for the gold. I can just say to you that it is here, and no mistake. I do not believe that any of the accounts that we saw before we left home were exag[g]erated. But there are a great many who make nothing. I should think that to take the population of the mining country, the average amount dug up per hand, would not be more than six or eight dollars per day. There are more men that I could hear of who made from one to three ounces per day than any other amount, and a man, I think, may safely calculate on that amount if he will work constantly. Some men have taken up as much as $2000 per day. One thing is certain, there is gold in the country. If I had 10 or $15000 I could make more gold at this place in twelve months than I would want. We arrived at a bad time; provisions have taken a rise and are still rising. Flour is now selling at $50 per barrel, and everything else in proportion. In the mining country a man can get $10 per day and board.

Yours, &c.

J. W. Bicknell.[4]

The optimism of these letters soon gave way to trouble and sorrow. Hugh Heiskell and Nelson Cannon contracted fevers, and in a few days both were dead. Tyler Heiskell wrote immediately to inform Hugh's parents of his death, but himself fell ill, as he explained to them in a letter a month later:

December 22nd 1849
Weaverville, California
My dear Uncle & Aunt

When I arrived, a month ago, from the City, I found Hugh dead. An opportunity (which is rare) presented itself and I had just time to announce the painful intelligence—intending in two days, at furthest of writing you the particulars, but I was myself, the next day, taken sick and have been confined to my bed & room ever since—today, being the first time I have left the house. I hope I may be able to finish this letter. Hugh, as I wrote, died the 16th of Nov. about 2 o'clock in the morning, after an illness of three weeks, though confined to his bed but about two. I did not see him during his illness, nor did I know but what he was well til I got back from Sacramento. The distance is 60 miles, and the means of communication in no regular way, and any message or note seldom reaches its destination. He had the Medical attention of Dr. White, whom I consider inferior to no other, but availed not to saving his life. The attention of a good nurse was wanting to some extent, though his friends who were with him did all they could—most of them being sick. I attended him tenderly in two more attacks crossing the plains—and am deeply sorry I was not here to nurse him in his last, for I know I could have added many comforts to his dying bed, but I could not—knowing nothing of it. I received a note from him, a week after I left, saying he had been sick, but was about again. He was conscious that his time had come for him "to depart hence and be no more on earth forever," and remarked but a short time before he expired, "Doc, I will die," and [that] is all he said. Though it is the severest affliction in human life, 'tis a consolation to christian parents to know and be assured, that an affectionate son, tho dead and far from his home & friends, was prepared to meet the dreaded hour. The God whom he vowed long since to serve, supported him, in many troubles & trials in a long & laborious journey across the "plains." The gentle and smooth temper, which particularly characterized him, when at home & in comfort & ease, seldom, if ever became unsmooth, during his long and tedious trip.

Abroad, as at home, all who knew him loved him, and associating for five months in a long journey, and necessarily in many ways—with a company of fifty people—all of whom were strange to him, he did not incur the displeasure, much less the ill-will, of any of them, and this can be said of but one other person of the company. We can say, but 'tis hard to feel "God's will be done."

If I could hear from you in less than three months, I would not dispose of anything he left, but it is possible we may not hear from you in six months and before that time will be compelled to do so. His clothing he left home with are almost all here—& as good as when he left. His part of the out-fit (wagon & team) we will account for and any thing else. Such things as he gathered to take home with him, we will carefully preserve, and bring with us should we return. We are in a house and located for winter, but at the breaking up of that season, we will go to the Mountains—and all a man can take with him, is what he can pack on his back or mule, if he is fortunate enough to have one—nor is there any place of safe deposit in this country, where only the kind branches of the oak offer a house during the dry season, hence you see the necessity of this course. I am about well of a severe attack of diarrhea, which weakened me much and was as severe a spell of sickness as I ever had. Col. Bicknell is also recovering from an attack of Typhoid Fever, taken at the same time I was.

Gold is more abundant than is represented in the States, anyone can make a fortune in 12 months, who has their health tho we have done but little more than pay expenses. Provisions are high. Flour here is worth $175.00 to $200.00 a barrel—Pork, the lowest, $200.00 per barrel, Fresh beef from 50 to 75 cts per pound—all considered cheap. In the city (Sacramento) Flour $45.00 per barrel. Pork 45 to 60 dollars per barrel. fresh butter $2.00 per pound.

Without any word or expressed wish, we will bring Hu's remains home should we be able so to do. Do not fail to write us immediately. If you should get this letter please inform them at home how we are doing. We are in a comfortable house, with plenty of provision for the winter & every thing necessary for our comfort.

Give my best love to the family & friends & may God bless you all.
Your Nephew,
Tyler D. Heiskell

P. S. Send all communications by New York & direct our friends to do the same. The Steamer frequently fails to call at New Orleans. Send to Sacramento City instead of San Francisco as before.[5]
T. D. H.

In her family history, Eliza Wallace said that her grandmother, Eliza Brown Heiskell, "never entirely rallied her energies after the death of her son Hugh," and died at fifty-four, more than a year after the news arrived from California. F. S. Heiskell was also hit hard, as he wrote to his friend John Bell:

You may have observed in the Knoxville papers the death of my son Hu. Oh! my kind friend, what a stroke was this. I had lost children before, and then I thought the cup of my affliction was full, for I thought it was impossible for man to feel any greater grief, any greater distress. I had wept over the graves of other near and very dear relatives and friends, but in humility I may say, how light were all these calamities compared to the loss of my noble Hu. He has left behind him few men of his age who were more promising, and none more spotless in character or more exemplary in deportment. But, I did not sit down to tell you of my anguish, tho' I know you will sympathise with me as a friend should feel.[6]

When Colonel Bicknell brought their winter supplies to Weaverville and found Hugh Heiskell and Nelson Cannon dead and Tyler Heiskell ill, he acted decisively but soon fell ill himself, as he wrote to Tyler's sister, who was caring for his two small daughters:

Ringgold, California,
April 11, 1850.
My Dear Sister:—It is long since I have written to you and still a longer time since I received a letter from Monroe. I have received three letters from Brother Temple, the last one dated June the 4th, neither Tyler nor myself have received a line from Monroe since we left home, and it now only lacks five days of one year. You can perhaps imagine how anxious we are to get a letter from some of you. If Brother Temple had not always mentioned you in his letters, we would be in perfect ignorance in regard to you all. He informs me in all of his letters that my dear Children were well and in good health and that relieved me greatly of anxiety.

You have long since received letters from Tyler stating the death of our dear friends and relations, Hu Heiskell and Nelson Cannon. Tyler and myself had both gone to Sacramento City to buy our winter provisions and I had kept on at the request of the boys to San Francisco, to get our letters if there were any, and never knew of their sickness until we heard of their death.

We have had quite a disagreeable winter owing to the frequent rains and snows. The snow soon melts away rarely remaining over two or three days, aside from the wet weather the winters are very pleasant in this country, the climate very mild never so cold as it is in East Tennessee.

We had a hard time of it during the winter. Tyler came up from the City and found that our dear friends Hugh and Nelson, had died during our absence. I remained and came up with the Wagon, a week after him; when I arrived I found not only our friends dead, but Tyler confined to his bed, in the tent with Diareah. As soon as I arrived and found Tyler sick, I determined to have a house for him and myself to winter in, cost what it would, so I turned out and in two days bought a comfortable cabin, and put him into it and he soon commenced mending and in two weeks was well.

The second day after we got into the house I was taken down with the fever, and was not able to rise for six weeks. Dr. White staid by us all the time and saved our lives, and Tyler as soon as he got able waited on me all the time, never leaving me for a moment that he could help. Since that we have both enjoyed better health than we ever did, and have been making some money. Tyler and Dr. White made April fools of us all by digging up a lump of pure solid gold weighing two pounds and a half and no mistake for I weighed it myself. It is the largest piece that has been found in this neighborhood, and created quite a sensation in our little Town. Tyler and Dr. White was working together that day as I was resting having walked myself down going to a Rancho, 10 miles off to hunt up a yoak of our cattle that was there. You can let the Monroe folks know that there is no humbug about that piece, for we intend bringing it home with us as we have got the Docts part in it by giving him other gold. The rainy season is pretty near over and we shall leave this place in a few days, for summer diggings. Mr. Howard left this morning with a company going to the south fork of the American fork of Sacramento rivers. Brown and Humphreys have been in the City of Sacramento all winter but we look for them up in a few days. Dr. White and Dick will go with Tyler and me wherever we go, they are living in a cabin about 100 yds from ours, both well.

California is now one of the most beautiful countries in the world, the whole face of it is covered with flowers of ever[y] hue that you can imagine. Tell our friends when they write to us hereafter to direct their letters to Sacramento City via New York. Write to me often and let me know how you all are and how my dear children are doing; enclosed I send each of them a piece of gold and two pieces for your self, one of them resembling very much the head of an old man.

Your affectionate Brother,

James W. Bicknell.[7]

Uncertainties and delays in the mail between the gold fields and the eastern states continued into the following year. It was seven months before Tyler Heiskell finally heard from his uncle and aunt and in turn explained to them that he had proceeded as he thought they would have wanted. He had sold Hugh's clothes and other possessions but retained some personal effects.

Weaverville Cal.

June 15, 1850

My dear Aunt

I returned to this place—home—last night—after an absence of three weeks, on a gold-hunting tour, and found a letter from you and cousin Margaret. Altho on a painful subject I was happy to receive a letter from you, who I love & esteem so much.

I have not received your first letter, and consequently have not done as you wished, but as my judgment dictated, with a proper sense of the feelings of the dearest relatives of my beloved deceased cousin, as I conceived.

I kept the watch—knowing the doubly melancholy value of it to you—also, the Greek & Latin Testament (which has your deceased brother's name in it), Hu's Bible, "A Mother's Gift," his Journal, a pistol presented to him by his brother Joseph, a silk purse & black silk cravat, all the pieces of rocks & wood gathered by him on our journey, five or six pieces, and a letter-folder, which I believe completes the list; I forgot, a pocket-book to carry bank-notes in & a gold pen, I also preserved. 'Tis hardly necessary to say, I did not expose my cousin Margaret's daguerrotype to sale. This, with the other things, I will preserve, if possible, and bring home with me, & be assured my dear Aunt, if we are able, we will bring Hu's remains home. Had

I known your wish, I would have endeavored, further, to have gratified it, but the reasons assigned in my letter are good, and you seem to be satisfied.

As to news, I have none to write, and gold-digging is too uncertain a business to calculate an hour or a foot ahead, but I can say, there is an abundance of gold here, but it will take an abundance of hard work to get it. There will be an immense amount of gold dug this season.

Provisions are cheaper now. By the mail which brought your letter, Colonel Bicknell received two, written in March. I have not rec'd a letter from home since Jany and only two since I have been in California, and they were from my dear mother. I don't think they have forgotten me, but blame the mails. With the Spring time I recovered my health & strength, and it never was better. The Colonel & myself will leave here in a few days for the Middle Fork to spend the summer digging gold. I will write to Father by the same mail that conveys this to you. I see by a letter from Vaughn to Brown, that there was an appropriation made to our Rail-Road, and that it would be completed, and I know the people are indebted to Father, for this Road, or the Appropriation and completion of it. We have not seen a word of the Tennessee Legislature and its adjournment. Nor have we seen the name of but five of its members, so you see there will be a blank leaf or two in the Book of Time of our allotment. I would rather see a Knoxville paper than find an ounce of gold, but have not seen one published in the last twelve months. The weather is delightful, and in a few weeks we will have people from the States, over-land, with us by the thousands. Nothing, Aunt, would give me greater pleasure than to receive a letter from you, when convenient for you to write, and also Uncle Frederick, which I think he can afford to do. I am sure Cousin Margaret will do so. My best love to the family—Cousin Ann and the Doctor. Colonel Bicknell joins in love to you all.

Your Nephew

Tyler D. Heiskell.[8]

Tyler Heiskell arranged for Cornelius Howard, when he returned to Tennessee, to take Hugh Heiskell's journal, and presumably the other items mentioned, back to his family. The diary was a unique memento of the lost son and brother, a record of his thoughts and experiences almost to the end. When Hugh made his last entry he had successfully passed the perils and hardships of the transcontinental crossing. At the outset of the journey he had written to his father of the "trip that may test, in more ways than one, the materials of which we are made."[9] He had reason to feel triumphant that he and his companions had been among the few who got their wagons all the way through to California. He had proved his mettle and he could face whatever lay ahead with confidence in himself and his abilities. He did not reckon with the debilitating effects of the journey on his constitution, or with the disease germs in a mining settlement where sanitation was little regarded. For Hugh Brown Heiskell, the golden dream ended 16 November 1849.

As for his companions, "the Monroe boys," J. W. Bicknell, Tyler Heiskell, Oliver White, and Dick White stayed in Weaverville during the winter of 1849–50, but with the coming of better weather they began prospecting for gold in fields to the north. Newspaper correspondents from East Tennessee spotted Tyler Heiskell and Colonel Bicknell at Nevada City on the Yuba River on 22 August; Tyler was seen there on 22 October, but by the thirtieth he had returned to Ringgold, where another correspondent located Bicknell and O. P. White.[10] A year after they arrived in California, Tyler Heiskell, Colonel Bicknell, Dr. White, and Richard White were still together.

Two years later, the Monroe boys were still keeping in touch to a certain extent, as Richard L. White showed when he wrote a letter to his father reporting the circumstances and prospects of kindred and friends in California.

Indian Dig[g]ings Calafornia
Nov the 13th 1852.
Dear Father

I feel it my duty to write to you to let you know how we are get[t]ing along in this country and something [of] our kindred and friends. We have been general[l]y in good health for the last twelve months and mining principal[l]y at this place our claims have paid a great deal of money but have not cleared much, on account of the dif[f]iculty in working them and bad management and extravigance of Cram Har[r]is but we have bought him out and have made about a thousand dollars in the last month clear which is the amount we paid him for his shair What we will do is verry unsertain but it is considered a verry valuable claim.

The Doctor has been prospecting about eight miles from this place and has struck some verry flat[t]ering prospects if [they] turn out as good as we antisipate we will come home in the spring.

[I?] have done nothing but mine since I came into the country have not made a dollar except that business The Doctor has traded in stock a good deel and would have made thousands of dollars if it had not been for the thiefs he has had ten thousand dollars worth of stock stolen from him since he commensed in the business He has on hand now a verry fine lot of cattle if he dont loose none will make considerable money.

Tyler Heiskell and Col Bicknell have been making money fast this summer. Jim Brown and John are not worth a cent. Anderson Humphreys is doing well. Wes McLemore kil[l]ed a man some two or three weaks ago and has escaped and there is a eleven hundred dollars reward offered for him he had the Small pox when he got away and is now laying out and is yet raw with scabs they will probibly get him off to night

I shall say nothing about politix for it has gone democratic by a s[m]all majority.

excuse me for not writing more frequent nothing more at present
Your affectionate Son
R. L. White[11]

Direct your letters to Sacramento City when you write to me.

Of the original group from Monroe County, Richard White omits mention of only Cornelius Howard, and he is known to have returned home from California carrying Hugh Heiskell's possessions back to his family. Exactly when that occurred is uncertain, but Cornelius Howard is listed in the Monroe County records as acting as the administrator of an estate in 1853.

With the passage of time, the traces become dim for almost all of the Monroe emigrants. In a letter to his younger brother Ewing White in 1857, Richard White implies that Oliver P. White is still in California, where Ewing joined them that same year. The three White brothers all stayed in California until 1860, when Oliver P. White abruptly left. It is not clear whether he was under indictment, but he was involved in the death of a man who had tried to destroy a dam White had built. After the incident, Dr. O. P. White returned east, married, and eventually joined the Confederate army. He died in July 1864, leading a charge near Martinsburg, West Virginia. A local historian records Richard White's death in California "some years later." A petition for the settlement of the estate of Cyrus A. Humphreys in 1875 mentions Anderson A. Humphreys as a resident of Monroe County. Because of the commonness of his name, John Brown disappears into anonymity in the public records.[12]

Colonel Bicknell and Tyler Heiskell, in contrast, stayed on in California for the rest of their lives, both enjoying a measure of material and political success. In 1860 Bicknell, having earlier abandoned his gold seeking to live for a while in Los Angeles, became county clerk of Amador County northeast of Sacramento. Four years later he moved to San Mateo, south of San Francisco, where he became a banker and was associated with Alvinza Hayward. In 1873 he was appointed county judge of San Mateo County, serving until his defeat in a bitterly contested election in 1880. While he occupied the bench he also owned a newspaper, the *People's Journal* of Mayfield, California. In 1882 he successfully ran for county clerk of San Mateo County, a post he held until his retirement in 1884. He is not known to have married again, but relatives joined him in California. His two daughters visited him after the completion of the transcontinental railroad, but they returned to Tennessee to resume their life with their aunt and foster mother, Mrs. Tipton. Bicknell spent his last years at the home of his sister, Mrs. William C. Blake, in Modesto, California, where he died in 1889.[13]

Tyler D. Heiskell, like Bicknell, became a permanent resident of California and enjoyed some success in politics. He was elected to the legislature from El Dorado County (the northern gold fields) in 1856. In the same year, he married Belle Patterson, formerly of Independence, Missouri, and originally from East Tennessee. Later, he established himself as a farmer and rancher on the Stanislaus River in what became Stanislaus County, where he was elected as a delegate to the state constitutional convention of 1878–79. In 1880 he was elected for a four-year term to the California Board of Equalization, which assessed large-scale corporate taxes.[14]

Toward the end of his life, Tyler Heiskell wrote to a cousin whom he had never met: "I left my father's home in Tennessee in 1849 for this State," he continued, "this then not a State." He went on to refer to his marriage and his three children, William King, Susan Patterson, and Jeff Davis, "a fine looking lot—the boys weighing 230 and 210 respectively." "The people of this glorious State have honored me above any merit I possess. I have served in the Legislature, a Member of the Convention that gave the State her present Constitution, the State Board of Equalization, and other minor positions." He hoped that one day his grown children would meet their cousins from the east, but he had become a Californian through and through and was content to stay at home, even though the cross-country journey had become relatively easy. Knowing so many of his childhood friends to be dead, he had lost the desire to return to the scenes of his youth.[15]

Of the nine companions who had set out together from Tennessee, five died in California. Of the remaining four, three went back to the eastern states, and the fate of the last is unknown. The two who achieved some prominence and prosperity may have acquired capital from their gold seeking, but their long-term California careers were based on banking and ranching, not gold mining. The seven Monroe boys who survived into the 1850s went their separate ways after the winter of 1849. There is no evidence that they ever reassembled. Yet, in memory, all of them, in California or back home in Tennessee, were bound together by the knowledge that for a few brief months they had been, as Hugh Heiskell named them in a letter to his father, a band of brothers in a great adventure.

Notes
. . . . .
PROLOGUE

1. For the general significance of the gold rush, readers should turn to works such as Malcolm J. Rohrbough, *Days of Gold: The California Gold Rush and the American Nation* (Berkeley and Los Angeles: Univ. of California Press, 1997); Paula Mitchell Marks, *Precious Dust: The American Gold Rush Era, 1848–1900* (New York: William Morrow and Co., 1994); J. S. Holliday, *The World Rushed In: The California Gold Rush Experience* (New York: Simon & Schuster, 1981); and John D. Unruh Jr., *The Plains Across: The Overland Emigrants and the Trans-Mississippi West, 1840–1860* (Urbana: Univ. of Illinois Press, 1979).

2. Tyler D. Heiskell to Mrs. Daniel List, 30 Oct. 1886; see also Eliza Brown Heiskell to Mary Ann Brown, 15 July 1833, and undated, microfilm no. 101, Genealogical Data, Tennessee State Library and Archives, hereinafter cited as Wallace Transcripts. Eliza Wallace copied many family letters and personal reminiscences into her genealogical records; Eliza Heiskell to Nancy Brown Lincoln, undated (1839?); same to same (Oct.? 1847), Heiskell-McCampbell-Wilkes-Steel Papers, Southern Historical Collection, Univ. of North Carolina, Chapel Hill.

3. Eliza Wallace, "A Bundle of Twigs," (unpublished family history), in editor's possession, 170–76.

4. Eliza Brown Heiskell to Frederick Steidinger Heiskell, 17 Nov. 1847, Wallace Transcripts.

5. Hugh Brown Heiskell to Margaret Heiskell, 8 Nov. 1847, Wallace Transcripts.

6. Eliza Brown Heiskell to Nancy Brown Lincoln (1840?), Heiskell-McCampbell-Wilkes-Steel Papers; obituary of Hugh Brown Heiskell, *Knoxville Register*, 2 Feb. 1850; Milton M. Klein (university historian, Univ. of Tennessee) to the editor, 22 Jan. 1992. Eliza Wallace, reminiscing, said that her uncle Hugh had been admitted to the bar, but as this was an event that happened before she was born, she was probably relying on family stories.

7. Frederick S. Heiskell to Eliza B. Heiskell, 6, 19 Oct. 1847, 9 Jan. 1848, Wallace Transcripts.

8. The editor is indebted to Neal O'Steen of Knoxville for details of Bicknell's enlistment.

9. Hall-Stakely Papers, East Tennessee Historical Center, Knoxville, 1830–31.

10. The medical department at Transylvania University was one of the larger institutions in the country offering a medical degree. The regular curriculum called for two years of lectures, with lessons in dissection an option. However, if an applicant had studied three years with a practicing physician, he might receive his degree after only one year's study. See Robert Peter, "The History of the Medical Department of Transylvania University," in *Filson Club Publication No. 20* (Louisville, Ky.: Morton and Co., 1908); Robert Peter, "Transylvania University: Its Origin, Rise, Decline and Fall," in *Filson Club Publication No. 11* (Louisville, Ky.: Morton and Co., 1896).

11. Clayton Reeve et al., "From Tennessee to California in 1849: Letters of the Reeve Family of Medford, New Jersey," ed. Oscar Osburn Winther, *Journal of the Rutgers University Library* 11 (1948), 33–84.

12. John Evans Brown, "Memoirs of an American Gold Seeker," *Journal of American History* 2 (1908): 30–31.

13. Advertisements that list steamboats, their captains, and schedules, *Knoxville Register,* 1849.

14. Louise Barry, *The Beginnings of the West: Annals of the Kansas Gateway to the American West, 1540–1854* (Topeka: Kansas State Historical Society, 1972), 807, 830, 850–65; J. Goldsborough Bruff, *Gold Rush: The Journals, Drawings and Other Papers of J. Goldsborough Bruff,* ed. Georgia Willis Read and Ruth Gaines (New York: Columbia Univ. Press, 1944), 2:439–45; Charles Edward Pancoast, *A Quaker Forty-Niner: The Adventures of Charles Edward Pancoast on the American Frontier,* ed. Anna Paschall Hannum (Philadelphia: Univ. of Pennsylvania Press, 1930), 172–76; *St. Louis Missouri Republican,* Apr.–May 1849.

15. Frederick Way Jr., *Way's Packet Directory, 1848–1983* (Athens: Ohio Univ. Press, 1983), 456; *St. Louis Missouri Republican,* 29 Apr., 2, 3, 8, 11, 16 May 1849.

16. For details of preparing for the journey, organizing a train, and developing the daily routines of travelers on a journey expected to last for months, see Merrill J. Mattes, *The Great Platte River Road: The Covered Wagon Mainline via Ft. Kearny to Ft. Laramie* (Lincoln: Nebraska State Historical Society, 1969). Insofar as the letters reveal, Hugh Heiskell's experience was typical.

17. For sabbatarian ideas and practices among the forty-niners, see Winton U. Solberg, "The Sabbath on the Overland Trail to California," *Church History* 59 (1990): 340–55. For Hugh Heiskell's own observance of the Sabbath, see the letter to his sister which follows.

18. Hugh Brown Heiskell? to Frederick S. Heiskell?, 17 May 1849, *Knoxville Whig,* 23 June 1849. The sender and the addressee are not identified by the newspaper editor.

19. Hugh Brown Heiskell to Susan Jacobs Heiskell, 20 May 1849, Heiskell-McCampbell-Wilkes-Steel Papers.

20. Hugh Brown Heiskell to Margaret Heiskell, 11 June 1849, Wallace Transcripts.

21. Perhaps from Capt. John McNulty's New York company, the Colony Guard, which Bruff locates in the vicinity at this time. See Bruff, *Gold Rush,* 1:467–69.

22. Hugh Brown Heiskell to F. S. Heiskell, 1 July 1849, Wallace Transcripts. Eliza Wallace wrote that the envelope containing this letter bore a notation: "Recovered from wreck of Steamer *Algoma*—burned at the wharf at St. Louis on the morning of the 29th of July 1849. Said boat had a large California mail—a large portion of which was entirely consumed. John M. Wimer, P. M."

23. For the legal complexities of mess and company organizations, see John Phillip Reid, *Law for the Elephant: Property and Social Behavior on the Overland Trail* (San Marino, Calif.: The Huntington Library, 1980), 132–66. For practical details of organizing a wagon train, see Henry Pickering Walker, *The Wagonmasters* (Norman: Univ. of Oklahoma Press, 1966).

24. Elisha Douglass Perkins, *Gold Rush Diary: Being the Journal of Elisha Douglass Perkins on the Overland Trail in the Spring and Summer of 1849,* ed. Thomas D. Clark (Lexington: Univ. of Kentucky Press, 1967), 22. For other references to Taplin, see William Brandon, *The Men and the Mountain: Frémont's Fourth Expedition* (New York: William Morrow & Co., 1955), 80; Charles H. Carey, ed., *The Journals of Theodore Talbot. 1843 and 1849–52* (Portland, Oreg.: Metropolitan Press, 1931), 7, 28, 47, 59; *Executive Documents,* 30th Cong., 1st sess., Doc. 1, serial 502, 1850, *Message from the President of the United States*; Francis B. Heitman, *Historical Register and Dictionary of the U. S. Army,* 2 vols. (Washington: GPO, 1903) 1:944; *New York Weekly Tribune,* 26 Sept. 1846; Jessie Benton Frémont, *Letters of Jessie Benton Frémont* (Urbana: Univ. of Illinois Press, 1993), 29; Barry, *The Beginnings of the West,* 644, 682–83, 687, 1167–69; James Madison Cutts, *The Conquest of California and New Mexico, by the Forces of the United States, in the Years 1846 & 1847* (Albuquerque: Horn & Wallace, 1965), 236.

25. Hugh Brown Heiskell to Frederick S. Heiskell, 17–19 May 1849, as printed in *Knoxville Whig,* 23 June 1849; *Missouri Republican,* 13 Aug. 1846; Charles G. Ellington, *The Trial of U. S. Grant: The Pacific Coast Years, 1852–1854* (Glendale, Calif.: Arthur H. Clark Company, 1987), 82; Cutts, *The Conquest of California,* 240.

26. Hugh Brown Heiskell to Frederick S. Heiskell, 17–19 May 1849, as printed in the

Knoxville Whig, 23 June 1849; Tyler D. Heiskell to William Heiskell, 5 Nov. 1849, as printed in the *Knoxville Whig,* 23 Feb. 1850; Hugh Brown Heiskell to Margaret Heiskell, 11 June 1849 and Hugh Brown Heiskell to F. S. Heiskell, 1 July 1849, Wallace Transcripts. See also diary entries for 5–21 October, when the train was breaking up.

27. Of the three, only Mrs. Thomas figures significantly in Hugh Heiskell's diary. For women forty-niners in general, see Joann Levy, *They Saw the Elephant: Women in the California Gold Rush* (Hamden, Conn.: Archon Press, 1990) and Mack Farragher, *Women and Men on the Overland Trail* (New Haven: Yale Univ. Press, 1979).

28. In his journal Hugh Heiskell makes repeated references to the black members of the Bicknell train. For blacks in the gold rush generally, see Rudolph Matthew Lapp, *Blacks in Gold Rush California* (New Haven: Yale Univ. Press, 1977).

29. The Donner party furnishes the prime example of the dangers of dissension on the trail. Quarrels over leadership and routes and finally a deadly encounter between two men caused delays that proved disastrous for many of the party and for some of their would-be rescuers in the snows of the Sierra Nevada. Charles Fayette McGlashan, *History of the Donner Party: A Tragedy of the Sierra* (Ann Arbor, Mich.: Univ. Microfilms, 1966), 34–38; George R. Stewart, *Ordeal by Hunger: The Story of the Donner Party* (New York: Henry Holt and Co., 1936), 63–65.

30. Bruff, *Gold Rush,* 2:22, 25.

31. See Unruh, *The Plains Across,* 101–4; Walker D. Wyman, "California Emigrant Letters," *California Historical Society Quarterly* 24 (1945): 42–43. The most complete account of the Pioneer Line is to be found in Bernard J. Reid, *Overland to California with the Pioneer Line: The Gold Rush Diary of Bernard J. Reid,* ed. Mary McDougall Gordon (Urbana: Univ. of Illinois Press, 1987), where Reid notes (p. 47) their arrival at Fort Kearny.

32. Irene Dakin Paden, *The Wake of the Prairie Schooner* (Gerald, Mo.: Patrice Press, 1985), presents a day-by-day account of the journey west, contrasting what the forty-niners saw with the modern landscape and locating camping spots near present towns. Though slightly dated, it is invaluable for anyone following the emigration, whether armchair or itinerant. Another useful compilation is Devere Helfrich, Helen Helfrich, and Thomas Hunt, *Emigrant Trails West* (Reno, Nev.: Trails West, 1984), which lists the markers erected by Trails West, Inc., at significant points, usually along the main highways. Excellent photographs along the trail in recent years are to be found in Greg MacGregor, "Traces of the Pioneers: Photographing the Overland Trail," *California History* 70 (winter 1991–92): 338–51.

1. Dent's "steamboat," a house wagon, was a precursor of the modern motor home. J. Goldsborough Bruff describes one belonging to the Alford family, who traveled with his company on the Lassen route. It had extensions built out beyond the wheels and contained a stove, whose pipe came out of the roof. The Alfords' "steamboat" housed three women and several children. Bruff, *Gold Rush*, 1:214–15.

2. Perhaps Lew Anderson, one of the lesser-known mountain men, who was located in the Bear River area in the late 1840s.

3. John Brown, one of the original group of emigrants from Monroe County, Tennessee, was roughly a contemporary of Hugh Heiskell.

4. Tyler Davis Heiskell (1823–1897), Hugh's cousin three years his senior, was the son of William and Elizabeth Heiskell, of Madisonville, Monroe County, Tennessee. William Heiskell farmed a considerable acreage with slaves and was currently a member of the Tennessee legislature. Tyler had graduated from Emory and Henry College near Abingdon, Virginia.

5. Such winnowing of their possessions was almost universal among the forty-niners, as Paula Mitchell Marks notes in *Precious Dust*, 69–70. John D. Lee made numerous expeditions from Salt Lake City along the trail to scavenge valuable items, which he took to Salt Lake for sale, as he relates in *A Mormon Chronicle, 1848–1876* (San Marino, Calif.: 1955).

6. "Squire" Elliott was perhaps one of the five unnamed associates whom Hugh Heiskell mentioned in a letter to his father as traveling with Capt. Dent.

7. Dr. Oliver P. White, one of the original Monroe County emigrants, was a young physician. He had attended East Tennessee University and then the medical department of Transylvania University in Kentucky. Accompanying him was his brother, Richard L. White.

8. Not mentioned in any of the letters that refer to the organization of the Bicknell train, Dr. Thompson may have been among those emigrants who were added to the nuclear group of the company at the mission, several days out from St. Joseph.

9. Andrew Humphreys, one of the original emigrants from Monroe County, was a contemporary of Hugh Heiskell's.

10. Alph Campbell's name appears only twice in the journal. He may have been a brother or son of Donald Campbell, who joined Bicknell's group at Florence, Alabama.

11. The *St. Joseph Gazette,* 18 May 1849, lists Alvarez among the Alabama contingent in Bicknell's train.

12. Jack Johnson was also listed in the *Gazette* among the Alabamians. In other references his name is coupled with Griffith, the presumed leader of mess number seven.

13. Aleck, or Alex, was a youthful slave belonging to Donald Campbell.

14. Overland travelers ordinarily followed the Green River south to Fort Bridger and then turned north toward Fort Hall on the Snake River. The Bicknell train, instead, took Sublette's Cut-off directly west when it reached Green River.

15. Richard L. White, also a Monroe Countian, the brother of Dr. O. P. White.

16. Nelson Cannon, a Monroe County emigrant, had been a fellow student of Tyler Heiskell's at Emory and Henry College; his brother married one of Tyler's sisters.

17. Probably John Brown of Columbia, Tennessee, who was Eliza Heiskell's half-brother.

18. Thomas L. ("Pegleg") Smith, a mountain man widely known for having amputated his own leg, had set up a trading post along the overland trail that was mentioned by nearly all diarists who passed that way. Exactly where the four log cabins stood remains uncertain. For biographical data, see Joseph J. Hill, "Ewing Young," *Oregon Historical Society Quarterly* 24 (1923): 6, 9, 10.

19. Bear River Valley has become farm country, divided between raising cattle and wheat.

20. Maj. W. D. Bassett was a member of the Campbell mess.

21. "Miss Lucy" must have been Mrs. Barnes; "Squire" Elliott belonged to Capt. Dent's mess. Hugh Heiskell seldom mentions Miss Barnes, the only young woman known to be in the train.

22. The Bicknell train was now traveling a newly opened route, Hudspeth's Cut-off.

23. Hugh Heiskell elsewhere calls Frank a "good, honest, clever Dutchman" but never gives his last name. He drove the wagon of Mr. and Mrs. Thomas.

24. In the only other reference to "Wilms," his first name is given as John.

25. See footnote 1.

26. As Hugh Heiskell notes, these men belonged to the second of the Pioneer trains, which left Independence several weeks after the Bicknell company departed from St. Joseph. In early June, the first train had passed them at or near Fort Kearny. For the Pioneer Line generally, see Bernard Reid, *Overland to California*; Unruh, *The Plains Across,* 101–4; Wyman, "California Emigrant Letters," 42–43.

27. The air pollution must have been widespread, for Bruff and Kimball Webster, who were seventy miles ahead on the trail, noticed the same phenomena at the same time. Webster said that a Mormon told him the Indians fired the grass to stop the emigrants

to California, but Frémont, in his description of the Humboldt country before it became a highway for gold seekers, asserts that it was customary for the Indians to burn the grass off in the fall. Indians sometimes did use grass fires as weapons, as Charles Taplin found out four years later when Apaches set fires that threatened the camp of Capt. John Pope's railroad exploration party. By setting backfires, Pope's men warded off the threat. John C. Frémont, *Geographical Memoir upon Upper California* (Washington, D.C.: U.S. Congress); Kimball Webster, *The Gold Seekers of '49* (Manchester, N.H.: Standard Book Co., 1917), 77–78; John Pope, *Diary of the Expedition [across Texas]*, House Executive Documents, 33d Cong., 3d sess., Doc. 91, 61.

28. Gen. Alexander Anderson, once a U. S. senator from Tennessee, organized a California train in East Tennessee that included some of Hugh Heiskell's contemporaries from Knoxville. Anderson's group was much more widely publicized than Bicknell's. Rather than wintering in Salt Lake City, Anderson and his company traveled to California by way of Santa Fe. See *Knoxville Register*, 30 May 1849; *St. Louis Missouri Republican*, 3 June 1849.

29. Hugh Heiskell's train had taken Hudspeth's Cut-off from Soda Springs to Steeple Rock, bypassing Fort Hall, the former Hudson's Bay post on the Snake River that had been taken over by the U. S. Army, and traveling more directly west to Steeple Rock, then south and west to the Humboldt River. The Mormon Road to which he refers ran from Salt Lake north and west to Steeple Rock and thence northward to the main trail from Fort Hall to Oregon.

30. The Morgan County and California Rangers. See *St. Louis Reveille*, 13 May 1849.

31. Presumably J. Goldsborough Bruff, commander of the Washington City Company. As noted in the prologue, the Bicknell and Bruff trains traveled only a few days apart on the trail and overlapped one another at times. However, Bruff does not identify the Bicknell train specifically.

32. John C. Frémont's name for the river, the Humboldt, has prevailed over the earlier Mary's River.

33. After a career as trapper and guide, Joseph L. Meek settled in the Willamette Valley of Oregon, where he became the U. S. marshal for the territory. He gained national attention when he brought the first Oregon constitution overland to Washington. O. P. and Richard White may have had a more personal knowledge of him and his brother from their uncle, who was also an early settler in the Willamette Valley.

34. On 16 May, C. D. De Camp, son of a St. Louis physician, saw some possessions of a friend being sold at auction to satisfy a debt. He attempted to intervene and received

a shoulder wound in the subsequent quarrel with the deputy sheriff. See *St. Joseph Gazette,* 18 May 1849; *St. Louis Reveille,* 23 May 1849.

35. In his use of "Dutch," Hugh Heiskell includes both ethnic German immigrants and Pennsylvania Dutch, but not necessarily Netherlanders.

36. The Bicknell train was camping near present-day Elko, Nevada, but the site cannot be located; the river has been channeled within cement walls and the marshes at the lower end of Ruby Valley have been filled in and built over, greatly altering the original terrain.

37. On this and the preceding page of the original journal the ink is quite faint, and someone has retraced the letters on this page with black ink. Since the last six lines are not retraced and are in what seems to be the same dark ink, Hugh Heiskell may have mixed some new ink and perhaps tried to make the preceding lines more legible.

38. "Razeeing" was the term for shortening both the bed and the wheelbase of a wagon.

39. Many emigrants turned west from the Humboldt River at a new "cut-off" called the Lassen route, which proved to be as arduous as and much longer than the Truckee River trail, which ran north of Lake Tahoe, or the Carson River trail, south of the lake.

40. Bruff, *Gold Rush,* 1:179, describes this trail post office, a barrel and accompanying bulletin board, where travelers left letters and notices for people who were following them.

41. At the Big Meadows (present Lovelock, Nevada) emigrants paused to rest, cut hay, and fill water barrels for the perilous trip ahead.

42. This was the wagon of Josiah Royce, with his wife, Sarah, and infant daughter, Mary, accompanied by three unattached forty-niners who had joined them. See Sarah Bayliss Royce, *A Frontier Lady: Recollections of the Gold Rush and Early California,* ed. Ralph Henry Gabriel (Lincoln: Univ. of Nebraska Press, 1977), 45–47.

43. Other travelers also used vinegar to neutralize the alkaline water; Alonzo Delano, *Life on the Plains and Among the Diggings* (Ann Arbor, Mich.: Univ. Microfilms, 1966), 87.

44. Probably a place known as Ragtown, so named because emigrants indulged in an orgy of bathing and washing after the desert ordeal, spreading their clothes to dry on every available bush. The Bicknell train apparently struck the Carson River some two miles closer to present downtown Fallon, Nevada. Residents of Fallon still occasionally make excursions up the desert trail in four-wheel-drive vehicles to hunt for remnants of items that emigrants abandoned.

45. In 1846 snows caught the Donner party attempting to cross the Sierra Nevada; when supplies ran out, some resorted to cannibalism.

46. The military governor of California, Gen. Persifer F. Smith, ordered army officers to

take provisions and draft animals to help the last emigrants over the mountains by all three major routes: Carson, Truckee, and Lassen. The government relief columns probably saved many lives in 1849.

47. Charles Sackett's train was the very last one to cross the Sierra Nevada by the Carson River route in 1849. See Charles Sackett to Robert W. Hunt, 7 Nov. 1849, U.S. Congress, Senate, *Message from the President of the United States,* 31st Cong., 1st sess., S. Doc. 52, 1850, serial 561.

48. The bare northeast face of Job's Peak.

49. Now known as Walley Springs. Around these springs David and Harriet Walley in 1862 built an elaborate spa with a ballroom and gardens. The present owners still cater to those who wish to "take the waters," but a twentieth-century hotel has replaced the original building, which burned in 1935.

50. The last two hundred yards below the summit are especially steep, with a gradient of 25 percent or more. Many of the trees now standing beside the trail might have been mature enough for the Bicknell train to use as anchors for ropes to relieve the strain on the oxen. Sarah Royce repeatedly mentions the steepness of the trail to Carson Pass, which caused difficulties even for her well-trained riding mule; Royce, *A Frontier Lady,* 68–72.

51. Hugh and Tyler Heiskell were fortunate in still having three of the four yoke of oxen they purchased in St. Joseph, for the Oregon-California trails were literally lined in places with the bones and carcasses of dead cattle; see Marks, *Precious Dust,* 69; Perkins, *Gold Rush Diary,* 121; Delano, *Life on the Plains,* 112, 192.

52. Lt. Robert W. Hunt. See the reports of Maj. D. H. Rucker, commander of the relief effort, and his subordinates in U.S. Congress, Senate, *Message from the President of the United States,* 31st Cong., 1st sess., S. Doc. 52, serial 561, 1850.

53. President Zachary Taylor appointed Gen. John Wilson as Indian agent for all the far western tribes, and Capt. Johnson as the sub-agent for California. They were escorted on their trip west by a detachment of the Mounted Rifle Regiment, which was currently moving cross-country to posts in Oregon. Only this small group came through by the Carson River route. Gen. Wilson took the Lassen cut-off and endured great hardships there.

54. Sarah Royce has the attack occurring on the night of the twenty-first; but her account was written years later and is thought to be based on a journal that has not survived. However, the details leave no doubt that they are reporting the same incident.

1. Reports of Maj. D. H. Rucker, commander of the relief effort, and his subordinates, U.S. Congress, Senate, *Message from the President of the United States,* 31st Cong., 1st sess., S. Doc. 52, 1850, serial 561.

2. Alonzo Delano, *Alonzo Delano's California Correspondence,* ed. Irving McKee (Sacramento, Calif.: Sacramento Book Collectors Club, 1952), 31; John S. Ross to a relative, 20 Jan. 1850, as printed in the *Knoxville Whig,* 6 Apr. 1850; David DeWolfe to Matilda DeWolfe, 12 Dec. 1849, *Transactions of the Illinois Historical Society* (1925): 217–18; see also Wyman, "California Emigrant Letters," 351–53, for letters about health and sanitary conditions written from Weaverville or its vicinity from October 1849 to March 1850.

3. Tyler D. Heiskell to William Heiskell, 5 Nov. 1849, from the *Knoxville Whig,* 23 Feb. 1850, reprinted from the *Athens Post.*

4. James W. Bicknell to his brother S. T. Bicknell, 10 Nov. 1849, printed in *Knoxville Register,* 16 Feb. 1850. See also James W. Bicknell, San Francisco, to E. E. Griffith, Madisonville, Tennessee, 10 Nov. 1849, in Reba Bayless Boyer, *Monroe County, Tennessee, Records, 1820–1877* (Athens, Tenn.), 2:154, repeating the same information.

5. In the early years of the gold rush no post offices existed in the rapidly shifting camps, and miners turned instead to the many private express companies that grew up to serve their needs, including picking up their mail in Sacramento or San Francisco; Roscoe Platt Conkling and Margaret B. Conkling, *The Butterfield Overland Mail, 1857–1869* (Glendale, Calif.: The Arthur H. Clark Co., 1947), 1:84–92; Oscar Osburn Winther, *Via Western Express and Stagecoach* (Stanford, Calif.: Stanford Univ. Press, 1945), 28–34. Outside the larger towns, the U. S. mail service remained unsatisfactory well into the 1850s.

6. Frederick S. Heiskell to John Bell, (draft), 6 Feb. 1850, F. S. Heiskell Papers, Archives, East Tennessee State Univ., Johnson City. Bell was a U. S. senator from Tennessee.

7. James W. Bicknell to My Dear Sister [Rachel Heiskell (Mrs. Q. A.) Tipton], 11 Apr. 1850, as printed in *Knoxville Whig,* 13 July 1850.

8. Tyler D. Heiskell to Eliza Brown Heiskell, 15 June 1850, Wallace Transcripts.

9. Hugh Brown Heiskell to Frederick S. Heiskell, 17–19 May 1849, as printed in the *Knoxville Whig,* 23 June 1849.

10. *Knoxville Whig,* 30 Nov., 21 Dec. 1850, 4 Jan. 1851.

11. Richard L. White to Thomas White, 13 Nov. 1852, photographic copy of manuscript letter in Richard L. White Letters, Archives, AR-36, Univ. of Tennessee, Knoxville.

12. Richard L. White to Thomas White, 13 Nov. 1852; J. I. Wright to O. P. White, 11 Apr. 1864; J. C. Vaughn to Dear Tom [White?], 31 July 1864, as printed in Boyer, *Monroe Records*, 2:146, 149–53, 158; Item no. 616, typed index of Monroe County records in the Madisonville Public Library, supplied through the courtesy of Adele Miller.

13. John G. Edmonds, "James W. Bicknell, County Judge, 1874–1880," *The Docket* 25 (Apr. 1990): 8.

14. Hubert Howe Bancroft, *History of California*, 6:698; 7:403, 409; *Knoxville Register*, 12 June 1856; *Memorial and Biographical History: Merced, Stanislaus, Calaveras, Tuolumne and Mariposa Counties, California* (Modesto, Calif.: McHenry Museum, 1980), 111.

15. Tyler D. Heiskell to Mrs. Daniel List, 30 Oct. 1886, Wallace Transcripts.

Bibliography
. . . . .

MANUSCRIPT SOURCES

Hall-Stakely Papers. East Tennessee Historical Center, Knoxville.

Heiskell, F. S. Papers. Archives, East Tennessee State Univ., Johnson City.

Heiskell, Hugh Brown. Diary of 1849. In private possession.

Heiskell-McCampbell-Wilkes-Steel Papers. Southern Historical Collection, Univ. of North Carolina, Chapel Hill.

Wallace, Eliza. "A Bundle of Twigs" (unpublished family history). In editor's possession.

Wallace, Eliza, comp. Genealogical Data. Tennessee State Library and Archives, Nashville. Microfilm.

White, Richard L. Letters. Archives, AR-36, Univ. of Tennessee, Knoxville.

. . . . .
NEWSPAPERS

Knoxville Register. 1836–60.

Knoxville Whig, 1849–51.

St. Joseph Gazette, 1849.

St. Louis Missouri Republican, 1849.

St. Louis Reveille, 1849.

San Francisco Alta California, 1849–50.

. . . . .
BOOKS AND ARTICLES

Abajian, James de T. *Blacks and Their Contributions to the American West.* Boston: G. K. Hall, 1974.

———. *Blacks in Selected Newspapers, Censuses and Other Sources.* Boston: G. K. Hall, 1977.

Bancroft, Hubert Howe. *History of California.* 7 vols. San Francisco: The History Co., 1884–90.

Barry, Louise. *The Beginnings of the West: Annals of the Kansas Gateway to the American West, 1540–1854.* Topeka: Kansas State Historical Society, 1972.

Boyer, Reba Bayless. *Monroe County, Tennessee, Records, 1820–1877.* 2 vols. Athens, Tenn.: privately published, 1969–70.

Brandon, William. *The Men and the Mountain: Frémont's Fourth Expedition.* New York: William Morrow & Co., 1955.

Brown, John Evans. "Memoirs of an American Gold Seeker." *Journal of American History* 2 (1908): 130–58.

Bruff, J. Goldsborough. *Gold Rush: The Journals, Drawings and Other Papers of J. Goldsborough Bruff.* Edited by Georgia Willis Read and Ruth Gaines. 2 vols. New York: Columbia Univ. Press, 1944.

Bryant, Edwin. *What I Saw in Calif./Rocky Mt. Adventures (Reprint).* New York: Appleton, 1848.

Buffum, E. Gould. *Six Months in the Gold Mines.* Edited by John W. Caughey. Los Angeles: The Ward Ritchie Press, 1959.

Carey, Charles H., ed. *The Journals of Theodore Talbot: 1843 and 1849–52.* Portland, Oreg.: Metropolitan Press, 1931.

Clark, Bennett C. "Diary of a Journey from Missouri to California in 1849." Edited by Ralph P. Bieber. *Missouri Historical Review* 23 (1928): 3–43.

Clark, S. B. F. *How Many Miles from St. Jo.* San Francisco: privately printed, 1929.

Conkling, Roscoe Platt, and Margaret B. Conkling. *The Butterfield Overland Mail, 1857–1869.* 3 vols. Glendale, Calif.: The Arthur H. Clark Co., 1947.

Cumming, John, ed. *The Gold Rush, Letters from the Wolverine Rangers to the Marshall Statesman, 1849–51.* Mt. Pleasant, Mich.: Cumming Press, 1974.

Cutts, James Madison. *The Conquest of California and New Mexico, by the Forces of the United States, in the Years 1846 & 1847.* Albuquerque: Horn & Wallace, 1965.

Delano, Alonzo. *Life on the Plains and Among the Diggings.* Ann Arbor, Mich.: Univ. Microfilms, 1966.

———. *Alonzo Delano's California Correspondence.* Edited by Irving McKee. Sacramento, Calif.: Sacramento Book Collectors Club, 1952.

Dewolf, David. "Diary of the Overland Trail and Letters of Captain David DeWolf," *Transactions of the Illinois State Historical Society* (1925): 183–222.

Downie, William. *Hunting for Gold: Reminiscences [!] of Personal Experience and Research in the Early Days of the Pacific Coast from Alaska to Panama.* San Francisco: California Publishing Co., 1893.

Edmonds, John G. "James W. Bicknell, County Judge, 1874–1880," *The Docket* 25 (Apr. 1990): 8.

Ellington, Charles G. *The Trial of U. S. Grant: The Pacific Coast Years, 1852–1854.* Glendale, Calif.: Arthur H. Clark Company, 1987.

Faragher, Johnny, and Christine Stansell. "Women and Their Families on the Overland Trail to California and Oregon, 1842–1867." *Feminist Studies* 2 (1975): 150 ff.

Faragher, Mack. *Women and Men on the Overland Trail.* New Haven: Yale Univ. Press, 1979.

Farnham, Elijah Bryan. "Diary." *Indiana Magazine of History* 46 (1950): 297–381, 403–20.

Frazer, Robert W. *Forts of the West: Military Forts and Presidios, and Posts Commonly Called Forts, West of the Mississippi River to 1898.* Norman: Univ. of Oklahoma Press, 1972.

Frémont, Jessie Benton. *Letters of Jessie Benton Frémont.* Urbana: Univ. of Illinois Press, 1993.

Frémont, John Charles. *Report of the Exploring Expedition to the Rocky Mountains.* Ann Arbor, Mich.: Univ. Microfilms, 1966.

Geiger, Vincent, and Bryarly Wakeman. *Trail to California: The Overland Journey of Vincent Geiger and Bryarly Wakeman.* Edited by David M. Potter. New Haven: Yale Univ. Press, 1945.

Gordon, Mary McDougall, ed. *Overland to California with the Pioneer Line: The Gold Rush Diary of Bernard J. Reid.* Urbana: Univ. of Illinois Press, 1987.

Hafen, LeRoy R., and Francis Marion Young. *Fort Laramie and the Pageant of the West, 1834–1890.* Glendale, Calif.: Arthur H. Clark Co., 1938.

Hafen, LeRoy R., ed. *The Mountain Men and the Fur Trade of the Far West.* 10 vols. Glendale, Calif.: Arthur H. Clark Co., 1965–72.

Heitman, Francis B. *Historical Register and Dictionary of the U. S. Army.* 2 vols. Washington, D.C.: GPO, 1903.

Herr, Pamela. *Jessie Benton Frémont: A Biography.* New York: F. Watts, 1987.

Hill, Joseph J. "Ewing Young." *Oregon Historical Society Quarterly* 24 (1923): 1–35.

Hine, Robert V. *In the Shadow of Frémont: Edward Kern and the Art of American Exploration, 1845–1860.* Norman: Univ. of Oklahoma Press, 1982.

Holliday, J. S. *The World Rushed In: The California Gold Rush Experience.* New York: Simon & Schuster, 1981.

Hughes, John T. *Doniphan's Expedition*. Chicago: Rio Grande Press, 1962.

Lapp, Rudolph Matthew. *Blacks in Gold Rush California*. New Haven: Yale Univ. Press, 1977.

Lee, John D. *A Mormon Chronicle, 1848–1876*. San Marino, Calif., 1955.

Levy, Joann. *They Saw the Elephant: Women in the California Gold Rush*. Hamden, Conn.: Archon, 1990.

——. "We Were Fortyniners, Too: Women in the California Gold Rush." *Overland Journal* 6 (1988): 29–34.

Marks, Paula Mitchell. *Precious Dust: The American Gold Rush Era, 1848– 1900*. New York: William Morrow and Co., 1994.

Mattes, Merrill J. *The Great Platte River Road: The Covered Wagon Mainline via Ft. Kearny to Ft. Laramie*. Lincoln, Neb.: State Historical Society, 1969.

McGehee, Micajah. "Rough Times in Rough Places." *Century Magazine* 41 (1891): 771 ff.

McGlashan, Charles Fayette. *History of the Donner Party: A Tragedy of the Sierra*. Ann Arbor, Mich.: Univ. Microfilms, 1966.

A Memorial and Biographical History: Merced, Stanislaus, Calaveras, Tuolumne and Mariposa Counties, California. Modesto, Calif.: McHenry Museum, 1980.

Morgan, Dale Lowell. *The Humboldt, Highroad of the West*. New York: Farrar & Rinehart, 1943.

Nash, Roderick. *Wilderness and the American Mind*. New Haven: Yale Univ. Press, 1967.

Nevins, Allen. *John Charles Frémont: Pathmarker of the West*. New York: Longmans, Green, 1955.

Paden, Irene Dakin. *The Wake of the Prairie Schooner*. Gerald, Mo.: Patrice Press, 1985.

Pancoast, Charles Edward. *A Quaker Forty-Niner: The Adventures of Charles Edward Pancoast on the American Frontier*. Edited by Anna Paschall Hannum. Philadelphia: Univ. of Pennsylvania Press, 1930.

Perkins, Elisha Douglass. *Gold Rush Diary: Being the Journal of Elisha Douglass Perkins on the Overland Trail in the Spring and Summer of 1849*. Edited by Thomas D. Clark. Lexington: Univ. of Kentucky Press, 1967.

Peter, Robert. "The History of the Medical Department of Transylvania University." In *Filson Club Publication No. 20*. Louisville, Ky.: Morton & Co., 1908.

———. "Transylvania University: Its Origin, Rise, Decline and Fall." In *Filson Club Publication No. 11*. Louisville, Ky.: Morton & Co., 1896.

Preuss, Charles. *Exploring with Frémont*. Edited by Erwin G. Gudde and Elizabeth K. Gudde. Norman: Univ. of Oklahoma Press, 1958.

Pritchard, James A. *The Overland Diary of James A. Pritchard*. Edited by Dale Morgan. Denver: F. A. Rosenstock, 1959.

Read, Georgia Willis. "Women and Children on the Oregon-California Trail in the Gold Rush Years." *Missouri Historical Review* 39 (1944): 1–23.

Reeve, Clayton, et al. "From Tennessee to California in 1849: Letters of the Reeve Family of Medford, New Jersey." Edited by Oscar Osburn Winther. *Journal of the Rutgers University Library* 11 (1948): 33–84.

Reid, Bernard J. Letter. *Western Pennsylvania Magazine of History* 44 (1961): 217–36.

———. *Overland to California with the Pioneer Line: The Gold Rush Diary of Bernard J. Reid*. Edited by Mary McDougall Gordon. Urbana: Univ. of Illinois Press, 1987.

Reid, John Phillip. *Law for the Elephant: Property and Social Behavior on the Overland Trail*. San Marino, Calif.: The Huntington Library, 1980.

Richmond, Patricia Joy. *Trail of Disaster*. Denver: Colorado Historical Society, 1990.

Rohrbough, Malcolm J. *Days of Gold: The California Gold Rush and the American Nation*. Berkeley and Los Angeles: Univ. of California Press, 1997.

Rolle, Andrew. *John Charles Frémont: Character as Destiny*. Norman: Univ. of Oklahoma Press, 1991.

Ross, Marvin Chauncey. *The West of Alfred Jacob Miller (1837) from the Notes and Water Colors in the Walters Art Gallery, with an Account of the Artist*. Norman: Univ. of Oklahoma Press, 1951.

Rotter, A. J. "Matilda for Gods Sake Write: Women and Families on the Argonaut Mind." *California Historical Society Quarterly* 43 (1979): 128–41.

Royce, Sarah Bayliss. *A Frontier Lady: Recollections of the Gold Rush and Early California*. Edited by Ralph Henry Gabriel. Lincoln: Univ. of Nebraska Press, 1977.

Shaw, R. C. *Across the Plains in Forty-Nine*. Edited by Milo Milton Quaife. Chicago: Riverside Press, 1948.

Solberg, Winton U. "The Sabbath on the Overland Trail to California," *Church History* 59 (1990): 340–55.

Stewart, George R. *The California Trail: An Epic with Many Heroes.* New York: McGraw-Hill, 1962.

———. *Ordeal by Hunger: The Story of the Donner Party.* New York: Henry Holt and Co., 1936.

Talbot, Theodore. *The Journals of Theodore Talbot, 1843 and 1849–52.* Edited by Charles H. Carey. Portland, Oreg.: Metropolitan Press, 1931.

Unruh, John D., Jr. *The Plains Across: The Overland Emigrants and the Trans-Mississippi West, 1840–1860.* Urbana: Univ. of Illinois Press, 1979.

U.S. Congress. House. John Pope, *Diary of the Expedition [across Texas].* 33d Cong., 3d sess. (1855). House Executive Document 91. Washington: U.S. Congress, 1855.

U.S. Congress. Senate. John Charles Frémont, *Geographical Memoir upon Upper California.* 30th Cong., 1st sess. Senate Document No. 148, Serial No. 511. Washington, D.C.: Wendell and van Benthuysen, 1848.

U.S. Congress. Senate. *Message from the President of the United States.* 31st Cong., 1st sess., S. Doc. 52, Serial No. 561. Washington: William M. Belt, 1850.

U. S. War Dept. *Reports of Explorations and Surveys to Ascertain the Most Practicable and Economical Route for a Railroad from the Mississippi River to the Pacific Ocean.* 13 vols. Washington: Beverley Tucker, et al., 1855–60.

Walker, Henry Pickering. *The Wagonmasters.* Norman: Univ. of Oklahoma Press, 1966.

Way, Frederick, Jr. *Way's Packet Directory, 1848–1983.* Athens: Ohio Univ. Press, 1983.

Weber, David J. *Richard H. Kern.* Albuquerque: Univ. of New Mexico Press, 1985.

Webster, Kimball. *The Gold Seekers of '49.* Manchester, N.H.: Standard Book Co., 1917.

Winther, Oscar Osburn. *Via Western Express and Stagecoach.* Stanford, Calif.: Stanford Univ. Press, 1945.

Wyman, Walker D. "California Emigrant Letters." *California Historical Society Quarterly* 24 (1945): 17–46, 117–38, 235–60, 343–64.

Index

· · · · ·